When
Counseling
Is Not
Enough

Discovery
House
PUBLISHERS

BOX 3566 · GRAND RAPIDS, MI 49501

*PUBLISHING BOOKS THAT FEED
THE SOUL WITH THE WORD OF GOD.*

When Counseling Is Not Enough

*Biblical Answers for
Those Who Still Struggle*

J. Kirk Johnston

Dedication

I dedicate this book to the memory of my grandparents: Kirk S. Lamb, Rena Bright Lamb, and William James Johnston, who encouraged me from childhood to live for Christ and whose lives were a beautiful example of Christian living.

I dedicate this book especially to my grandmother, Fern Autumn Johnston, who was among the first to believe that God would use me for His glory, and who prays daily for me to this end. Thank you, Grammy. I love you.

When Counseling Is Not Enough
Biblical Answers For Those Who Still Struggle
Copyright © 1994 by J. Kirk Johnston

Unless otherwise indicated, Scripture is taken from the
NEW AMERICAN STANDARD BIBLE.
Copyright © 1960, 1962, 1963, 1968, 1971, 1972, 1972, 1973, 1975, 1977,
by The Lockman Foundation.

Discovery House Publishers is affiliated with
Radio Bible Class, Grand Rapids, Michigan 49501

Discovery House books are distributed to the trade
by Thomas Nelson Publishers, Nashville, Tennessee 37214.

ISBN 0–929239–79–2

Printed in the United States of America

94 95 96 97 98 99 / CHG / 10 9 8 7 6 5 4 3 2 1

Contents

Acknowledgments

Solomon wisely observed, "There is nothing new under the sun. Is there anything of which one might say, 'See this, it is new?' " (Ecc. 1:9–10). And this is also true with this book. Nothing I have written here is original with me; many mentors have influenced my thinking. Two stand out.

The first does not even know me personally, but for years I have read his books, and my appreciation for him has grown with each new publication. Much of my counseling theory and methodology have been borrowed from him. The person I am referring to is Larry Crabb, and I am heavily indebted to this godly counselor.

The other man is Neil Anderson. It was my privilege to study with him while I did my doctoral work. Neil opened my eyes to many important aspects of spiritual warfare, counseling, and discipleship. Without him I might still be in the dark on many crucial truths. I thank God for this man's influence in my life as well.

But no human mentor has the influence on me that God's Word has. I am in awe of its complete trustworthiness and accuracy down through the centuries as well as its incredible relevance for today. And though I often agree with godly people, I am quick to disagree when someone contradicts any portion of Holy Scripture. My most important mentor and my final authority is God's Word. If I am mistaken in any given area of my thinking, it is not because I have slavishly followed a mere mortal, but because I have misunderstood what the Bible actually teaches. My hope and prayer is that nothing in this book is original with me but that everything written here has ultimately come out of God's Word (2 Tim. 2:15).

When it comes to people who have been helpful during the process of writing this book, I have to say that it has been a delight to work with Tim Beals. As my editor, he first gave me wise counsel about what to include in the book, and then he worked on it as if it were his own. Thanks, Tim, for your wisdom and gentleness.

Once again Dr. Robert DeVries and Carol Holquist went out on a limb by entrusting me with a very delicate and important subject. Your faith in me is very much appreciated.

Barb Allen came on as my personal assistant near the end of this project, but her help was invaluable. Barb, thanks for all your hard work.

I want to thank all the people of Harmony Bible Church, especially the elders, for giving me a sabbatical. That time was very important for me and my family and it contributed heavily to the completion of this book. Blessings on all of you.

I also would like to thank the Pastoral Counseling class I taught at Tampa Bay Theological Seminary. Many of the concepts and principles included in this book were presented to you and your feedback made them better.

How can I sufficiently thank Tim Jackson for writing the foreword to this book. That act of kindness, along with his encouraging words has really impressed me. He is the kind of person I would go to for help, and many people have. God bless you in your counseling ministry.

Last, and most important, I want to thank my wife, Gayle. She is the one who most encouraged me to do this book. She knows all of my sins, weaknesses, and shortcomings, and yet she is unfaltering in her belief that God can use me to help hurting people. She also put the entire manuscript on computer—more than once—and endured my constant tinkering with the manuscript. In addition she gave valuable input about the content and direction of this book. She constantly reminded me that struggling people need to be pointed toward Jesus Christ more than anything else. Gayle, next to eternal life through Jesus Christ, you are God's greatest gift to me and I am eternally grateful.

Publisher's Foreword

For quite some time I have been concerned over what I have come to believe is a growing overdependence upon counseling in our society. And the church is no different.

I felt uncomfortable recently when I heard one of my client's say, "Well, what would Tim say about this?" as though I were the final authority on the way she should live her life. Instead, what I long to hear my clients say is "What would God say about this?"

Through counseling, relationships can be improved, and people's lives can change. However, I agree with Kirk Johnston that unless we as counselors move people toward the goal of becoming more God-dependent and Christlike in the way they handle every aspect of their lives, then we are guilty of treating the wounds of God's people superficially (Jeremiah 8:11).

In *When Counseling Is Not Enough,* Kirk demonstrates the need for counseling, not as a cure-all, but as one of several critically important weapons in the arsenal of the local church for helping individuals who are struggling.

Kirk demonstrates the need to combine counseling with ongoing discipleship and a caring community within the local church to bring about change in people's lives for good. As a counselor myself, I long for the partnership the author describes with the pastors of the churches whose people I counsel.

I appreciate Kirk Johnston for several reasons. First, as a pastor, he sees his shepherding role not as being confined to the proclamation of the truth from the pulpit (as vitally important as I believe that is). He is willing to get involved in the nitty gritty details of the struggles of life of his parishioners. He's real.

Second, Kirk does not pretend to be an expert on the issues of depression, addictions, abuse and other such major struggles that confront every pastor who gets involved with his people. However, it is obvious that he has taken the time to read widely and to become better informed about these issues so that he can be as helpful as possible to the people he deeply cares about.

Third, Kirk has taken time not just to respond to different counseling models or positions, but he has attempted to strike a delicate balance throughout this volume. I support his "holistic" view of people that acknowledges the interrelatedness of every person's physical, emotional, rational, relational, and spiritual being.

Fourth, I appreciate Kirk's strong chapter on the use of the Scriptures in counseling. I share his concerns for the counseling done by many well-meaning Christians that has no foundational basis in the Scriptures.

Finally, the warm style that is evident throughout Kirk's book exposes the reader to his heart for God and his love for people who are struggling. I would be honored to work as a counselor alongside a pastor who evidences this much compassionate care, informed understanding, and deep conviction about helping others grow to become the men and women God has designed them to be.

Tim Jackson
Senior Counselor,
Radio Bible Class

Part 1

1. When Counseling Is Not Enough

WHEN I told some friends I was writing a book on counseling, they took me aside to tell me "their story." It began many years before when the husband, a Christian, became seriously depressed. The couple went first to their pastor for help. The pastor was a man who not only believed the Bible was completely true, he also believed that the Bible was sufficient to address every human problem. Yet for some reason he told the couple that he was unable to counsel the depressed man.

A little bewildered, the couple then sought help from a Christian psychologist. Unable to find help from the psychologist, they went next to a Christian psychiatrist. But neither of these counselors provided the necessary help for the struggling husband. Finally, in desperation, the couple went outside the Christian community to a state-employed psychologist. The support from this counselor was barely sufficient, but the help they got was better than any they had received from Christian professionals. This incident strengthened my resolve to write this book.

My first reaction to this account was sorrow. I felt bad for these people who so desperately needed and wanted guidance, but had to work so hard just to get help that was merely adequate. My second response was anger and disappointment with those who had apparently failed these believers. But I was aware from my own counseling experience and research that many Christians who seek help today do not find it.

I want to be as clear as possible about the purpose and audience of this book. My desire in these pages is not to address Christian counseling professionals, but rather to encourage ordinary, hurting Christians who have sought counseling or therapy and yet continue to struggle.

More specifically, I am writing to believers who have received counseling, perhaps extensively, and yet have not made much discernible progress in dealing with their problems. I am also addressing Christians who, through counseling or therapy, have overcome many of their problems, but cannot seem to get to a point of wholeness in their lives.

I realize that life, even for Christians who experience a measure of maturity and success, can be very difficult and painful. I also recognize that there are few problems today that can be fixed quickly or easily. Nevertheless, I firmly believe that more can be and should be done to help Christians who want and need it.

My most immediate desire is to say to those who still struggle, there is *hope*! Please do not give up on all counseling professionals. Please do not give up on yourself. And most importantly, please do not give up on God! He does love and care about you. He is aware of your frustrating and painful situation and He wants to help. As Jeremiah 29:11 says, "'I know the plans that I have for you,' declares the LORD, 'plans for welfare and not for calamity to give you a future and a hope.'"

Even though this is a promise made specifically to the nation Israel, it still has a very real application for believers today. This same God still has the desire and a plan to help you.

This book will help unfold that plan. In it I hope to explain why some counseling is inadequate and why most people require more than simply counseling. Beyond these explanations, I believe that this book will provide biblical help and direction for Christians who want to seriously address the problems and issues in their lives. Many struggling believers have complex problems that need to be addressed in a variety of ways. But ultimately, I want to show that nothing of any value will be accomplished unless people have a fresh encounter with the living God and trust Him like they never have before.

So if you are serious about dealing with your problems and strongly desire to get better, I invite you to explore with me what has gone wrong and how things can begin to go right!

2. The Issue of Physical Problems

TIM Jackson, who directs the counseling ministry for Radio Bible Class, relates this true story in his booklet, *When Help Is Needed*:

> I once had a woman come to my office complaining of a severe battle with depression. It sapped her vitality for living to the point that she was unable to function at home and care for her three preschool children. Thoughts of suicide plagued her daily activities. She had just been released from a three-week stay at a hospital mental health unit and reported that the psychological therapy had made very little difference. Her husband was totally frustrated with her and was at his wits' end.
>
> After several extended conversations with her, which seemed to be equally unhelpful, I asked her when she had her last complete physical. As we discussed her

health, she had mentioned that she felt as though she was "losing her mind." She had hot flashes and then was extremely cold within minutes. Her menstrual cycle was erratic.

She had all the symptoms of a woman going through menopause. But that didn't seem possible. She was only 34. I asked when her mother went through menopause. She said at 32. And her grandmother? Her early 30s. But because she didn't fit the normal profile for a woman going through menopause, all doctors she had visited had consistently ruled it out.

She made an appointment with a new gynecologist, who performed some specific tests and found that she had the estrogen level of an eighty-year old woman! Soon after she started estrogen hormone therapy, her depression lifted. All the counseling in the world would have only frustrated her because she had no control over how her body was responding.[1]

When a person has been receiving counseling or therapy and is not really making progress with his or her problem, the primary issue may not be spiritual or emotional, but physical. Some people go for a complete physical exam before they go to a counselor. Some counselors insist on a physical exam before they will begin counseling anyone. This is not always necessary, but counselors and counselees need to be open to the possibility that in any given situation the root problem could be physical. It is unfortunate that even today there are many Christians and some Christian counselors who refuse to acknowledge this possibility. Some Christian counselors and pastors still believe that all emotional difficulties are a direct result of personal sin. While I admire their willingness to accept sin as a frequent cause of emotional distress, I am concerned that these professionals may unnecessarily increase the pain of hurting people instead of helping to relieve it.

I know a woman who suffers from bipolar depression. This is a hereditary disorder that is often passed on from generation to generation. It causes a person to experience extreme mood swings from incredible highs to unbelievable lows. It does not have as much to do with one's spiritual beliefs as it does with certain chemicals lacking in the brain. For years many well-meaning people urged her to read the Bible and ask God for help to cope with her problem. People were extremely frustrated with her and she felt terrible guilt when all her spiritual efforts failed to produce any substantial change in her feelings or behavior. Now she takes medication for her problem and is able to live in a much more normal and God-honoring manner. There are many others like her who need to see a doctor; but someone has told them that if they just "get right with God" or "adjust their attitude" everything will be fine. This is tragic.

But there are two issues here: it's one thing for a troubled Christian to forego a visit to the doctor because he or some other well-intentioned layperson thinks that his problem is entirely spiritual; it's another matter altogether when a pastor or Christian counselor refuses to refer this hurting person to a medical doctor. This is gross negligence. If there is any doubt about the root source of a counselee's problem, or if a counselee fails to make discernible progress, the counseling professional is obliged to bring a doctor into the situation.

I will never forget being in the living room of a woman who was apparently under satanic attack. She was stretched out on a couch and her whole body was convulsing. Her complaint, as she cried out, was that she felt she was going to die. Worse yet, she wasn't sure she was a believer who would go to heaven. She thought she was going to hell.

I attempted to calm her down by reassuring her of her salvation based on her confession of faith in Christ and the confirming work of the Spirit in her life. However, her serious doubts persisted.

At this point, I pursued the very real possibility that she was being oppressed by a demon. I had her pray a "warfare prayer" designed to help me discern whether or not there was demonic involvement in her life. The prayer was also to help her combat any forces of darkness that might have been attacking her. She prayed the prayer without any hesitation, flinching, or adverse reaction whatsoever. At the same time, she continued to complain about doubts, fears, and physical problems.

After inquiring from her husband about what medical attention, if any, she had received, I was assured that she had been thoroughly examined by a doctor who gave her a clean bill of health. But, because of the severity of her situation, I recommended that she be reexamined. I had to believe that there was a physical cause for her emotional and spiritual distress. Shortly thereafter the couple went to another doctor who did, in fact, find a major physical problem. This woman had a heart condition which, as it turned out, was a primary cause of her distress and doubts.

The point is that sometimes a person has a physical malady that leads to or contributes to emotional problems. Christians and counselors need to be willing to accept and pursue that possibility. At the same time, it is important to understand that in many cases, believers have spiritual/emotional problems that can lead to physical difficulties.

In Psalm 32:3, David says,

> When I kept silent about my sin, my body wasted away
> through my groaning all day long . . . .

The Bible is clear that unresolved sin can lead to serious physical consequences. When this is the case, the afflicted individual has to be willing to acknowledge sin and seek forgiveness to receive physical healing (James 5:15–16).

One example of this truth is found in the book *Occult Bondage and Deliverance* by Kurt Koch. The author tells of a rapidly dying woman who summoned a Christian man to her bedside. Then for over two hours she confessed her sins to him. When she was done confessing, she felt she was ready to meet her Maker. However, she didn't die; in fact, she got well. God had healed her in response to her confession, even though she hadn't asked for healing.[2]

Thus counselors need to be willing to work with medical doctors, and doctors need to be open to work with counselors. In many cases it is difficult to tell whether a physical disorder has led to an emotional one or vice versa. A counselee's situation often needs to be addressed from both a physical and a spiritual perspective to bring about complete restoration and healing.

The sad fact is that some counselors are unwilling to refer clients to physicians, but even if they do, physicians are sometimes unwilling to cooperate with the counselor as a partner in treatment.

Not long ago I advised a counselee to check into a hospital temporarily for medical treatment of his depression. When I called the attending physician to speak with him about the situation, he very politely but firmly told me that this was none of my business and that I was out of my area of expertise. This happens all too frequently. Fortunately, there are doctors who will cooperate with Christian counselors in the healing process.

Having explained the need in some cases for medical treatment as well as counseling, an important question arises: Is there such a thing as mental illness?

Some, even in the fields of psychology and psychiatry, would say no.[3] Jay Adams calls mental illness a "misleading misnomer."[4] Nevertheless, even he is willing to admit that "organic malfunctions affecting the brain that are caused by brain damage, tumors, gene inheritance, glandular or chemical disorders, validly may be called mental illness."[5]

In other words, if one's thoughts, feelings, or behavior are abnormal because of an actual physical problem in the brain, one has a mental illness. But if one's problems are not caused by physical difficulties, that person has a spiritual/emotional problem and that condition should not be called "mental illness."

A person who has a mental illness needs medicine and/or surgery and should be under a physician's care. However, if the person has a spiritual/emotional problem, no matter how severe, a trained counselor using scriptural principles will be able to help this individual. A good example of this fact is given in Adams' book *Competent to Counsel*:

> Steve was a young man of college age whom the writer met in a mental institution in Illinois. Steve had been diagnosed by psychiatrists as a catatonic schizophrenic. He did not talk, except minimally, and he shuffled about as though he were in a stupor. Upon sitting down, he became frozen in one or two positions. At first, communication with Steve seemed impossible. He simply refused to respond to questions or to any kind of verbal overtures. However, the counselors told Steve that they knew he understood fully what was going on, that though he might have fooled others—the psychiatrist, his parents, the school authorities—he was not going to fool them. They assured Steve that the sooner he began to communicate the sooner he'd be able to get out of the institution. Steve remained silent, but was allowed to continue as a part of the group observing the counseling of others. The next week the guns were turned on Steve, and for more than an hour the counse-

lors worked with him. Steve began to break down. His hesitant replies gave evidence that he clearly understood everything. There was no reason to believe that he had withdrawn from reality.

As Steve began to respond, the rough outlines of his problem emerged. But the third week he broke down entirely. Steve had no mental disorders. Steve had no emotional problems. Nothing was wrong with his mind and emotions. His problem was autogenic. Steve's problem was difficult but simple. He told us that because he had been spending all his time as prop man for a play rather than working at his college studies, he was about to receive a raft of pink slips at the midsemester marking period. This meant that Steve was going to fail. Rather than face his parents and his friends as failures, Steve camouflaged the real problem. He had begun acting bizarrely, and discovered that this threw everyone off track. He was thought to be in a mental stupor, out of touch with reality—mentally ill.

The truth was that Steve was hiding behind the guise of illness in much the same way that a grammar school child will feign illness when he doesn't want to take a test for which he has not prepared adequately. Steve had done this sort of thing many times before, but never quite so radically. At times he would go off by himself and grow quiet and still and become hard to communicate with, and at other times he would walk off down the road and wouldn't return for hours. Over the years Steve gradually had developed an avoidance pattern to which he resorted in unpleasant and stressful situations. When the college crisis arose he naturally (habitually) resorted to this pattern. Steve's problem was not mental illness, but guilt, shame, and fear.[6]

Summary

Some people are indeed "mentally ill," but not everyone who appears to be truly is. But even struggling Christians who are not mentally ill often need a physician's care and perhaps medication to address their problems adequately. However, as Frank Minirth points out,

> The basic [spiritual/emotional] problems must still be dealt with in order to really help the patient. The medications serve to help the patient become mentally functional through balancing the biochemistry of the brain so that the patient can then progress in therapy.[7]

So, medical help is often required when the root problem is physical, or even when spiritual/emotional problems have led to physical difficulties. However, if the basic issues are spiritual/emotional, even if there are physical symptoms, as soon as the spiritual/emotional problem is adequately addressed, the physical symptoms usually begin to disappear. Unfortunately, one common problem is that many struggling Christians go for counseling and the counselor addresses the emotional aspect of the problem, or the spiritual dimension, but not both. This is a common situation when counseling is not enough. And it is this problem we will discuss in chapter 3.

Questions for Reflection and Action

1. Do you have any physical problems that have accompanied your spiritual/emotional distress? If so, have you mentioned them to your counselor?

2. Have you seen a medical doctor about your physical symptoms? If not, is it because you are concerned about going or because your counselor has discouraged it?

3. Have you encouraged your counselor and doctor to work together to help you, and have you signed the necessary releases that will allow them to do so?

4. Have you shared your physical symptoms with your extended family to explore the possibility of a hereditary physical problem?

5. If your doctor and counselor have not been able to determine the primary cause of your problems, have you considered seeing another doctor or specialist?

Notes

[1]Tim Jackson, *When Help Is Needed.* Grand Rapids, MI: Radio Bible Class, 1993, pp. 6–7.
[2]Kurt Koch, *Occult Bondage and Deliverance.* Grand Rapids, MI: Kregel, 1972, p. 75.
[3]See Thomas Szasz, *The Myth of Mental Illness.* New York: Dell, 1960.
[4]Jay Adams, *Competent to Counsel.* Grand Rapids, MI: Baker, 1970, p. 28.
[5]Ibid.
[6]Ibid., pp. 31–33.
[7]Frank Minirth and Walter Byrd, *Christian Psychiatry.* Old Tappan, NJ: Revell, 1990, p. 147.

3. Emotional and Spiritual Problems

RECENTLY a very distraught mother came to see me about her son. He had been threatening to kill himself for some time, but the mother did not take the suicide notes and verbal threats seriously. She did not believe that he truly intended to commit suicide. Finally, however, she woke up to the fact that her son desperately needed counseling, even if he wasn't serious about taking his own life. She took him to a "Christian" counselor. The boy hit it off well with the counselor from the very beginning. He actually enjoyed going to counseling! The problem was that the boy almost always left his counseling sessions feeling very good about himself and better about his situation, but the good feelings didn't last. Within a day or so after a counseling session, he was back to littering the house with suicide notes. He wasn't really making progress but he truly liked his counselor and did not want to stop meeting with him. This was what concerned the mother so much. Her son was not getting better, but she was frightened to suggest that he quit counseling. She was afraid that severing this relationship might push him over the edge. And she came to me for help to determine why her son's counseling was not more effective and what she should do about it.

You may find yourself in a similar situation. Perhaps you have been going to a Christian counselor and you sense that the counselor is genuinely concerned about you. You feel loved and accepted and you leave your counseling sessions feeling good about your counselor, yourself, and your situation. But your good feelings do not last very long and you realize that you are struggling as much as ever with your personal problems. How can things end up so wrong when they start out feeling so right?

It is important for the counselor to address a client's emotions. After all, our emotions are a God-given part of our makeup as human beings. God has emotions (Eph. 4:30) and He has created us in His own image (Gen. 1:27). However, the reason and manner in which counselors address one's feelings is crucial. Minirth correctly states that "it is important to realize that although feelings are extremely important and should be listened to, most individuals have very little direct control over changing their feelings."[1]

It is true that one cannot simply decide to change the way one feels. That is why it is ineffective to simply tell someone, "You shouldn't feel that way." But it is equally ineffective to simply urge one to feel better, though many counselors do so anyway. The truth is that only a sustained change in thought and behavior will lead to a significant change in the way a person feels.

But what if one is not motivated to change the way one thinks or behaves? Some are not willing to change their thought or behavior patterns even when they know that their current patterns are either dysfunctional or self-destructive.[2]

In these cases, it is as useless to simply tell these people to "just stop thinking about it" or "just do it" as it is to tell them "you shouldn't feel that way." To effectively help unmotivated believers, there must often be an appeal to their emotions, not simply a plea for them to feel, think, or act differently.

In Romans 12:1, Paul urges the Roman Christians to give their lives in service to God on the basis of "the mercies of God," that is, on the basis of what God had done for them. He precedes this plea with eleven chapters that outline and explain how wonderful God's mercy has been toward them. There is no doubt that Paul is appealing to the minds of his readers, but he is also attempting to touch their emotions. He says in Romans 5:6–8,

> While we were still helpless, at the right time Christ
> died for the ungodly. For one will hardly die for a righ-
> teous man; though perhaps for the good man someone
> would dare even to die. But God demonstrates His own
> love toward us, in that while we were yet sinners, Christ
> died for us.

Paul wants to touch his readers emotionally and move them toward acceptance of proper thought and behavior. There is nothing wrong with an emotional appeal that is appropriate and truthful. In fact, in counseling this is necessary at times to motivate people to think and act correctly. But sometimes even an appropriate emotional appeal is not enough to get people going in the right direction.

When a person feels unloved, unaccepted, and perhaps rejected or abused, that person is not likely to respond quickly or easily to counseling. The counselor is going to have to gain that person's trust, often through empathy. Gary Collins defines empathy as a "sensitivity to the hurts and needs of others and a willing attempt to see and experience the world from the other person's perspective."[3] One will first want to know that the counselor understands one's feelings and cares about one as a person. It's like the saying goes, "People do not care how much you know until they know how much you care." Until the counselor communicates that he or she understands and cares, the client may be unwilling to listen, let alone to change. But when the counselee has felt love and understanding there will be motivation for both real listening and change.

A problem with some Christian counseling is that the counselor makes contact with the client on an emotional level and gains the client's trust. But then the counselor fails to use that trust as a motivation for change. Why?

After sharing the hurt and pain of one who has been emotionally and/or physically traumatized, counselors may be reluctant to insist on change. The counselor may begin to believe that the counselee has been so traumatized as to be "psychologically unable" to do what is necessary and right, and that the "loving" thing to do is not to strongly urge right thinking and behavior. But the "loving thing to do" after the counselee is convinced that the counselor cares is to insist that he or she do what is necessary for healing and growth. Not to do so is unloving and is like throwing a lifeline to a drowning person but then failing to pull in. Empathizing is often the loving thing to do to in the beginning. But when the client knows that the counselor cares, then empathy must be augmented with encouragement, and even insistence upon right thinking and right behavior.

There is another way that empathy can impede the process of healing. Some time ago I saw an advertisement for a Christian recovery clinic. The clinic's slogan was "We won't judge you, just love you." The implication is that if the counselor loves the counselee no judgments will be made. This is a dangerous conclusion which sometimes comes from empathy.

When the counselor empathizes with the struggles and problems of the counselee, one can easily come to the conclusion that under similar circumstances he or she would probably react the same way. And the counselor should probably share that with the counselee. Nevertheless, just because one understands, humanly speaking, why one acts the way one does, this does not mean that one should remain silent. Empathy should not prevent healing from taking place, but it sometimes does.

Some counselors recognize the importance of addressing what a struggling believer feels. But unless the counselor is willing to move on to why the person feels a certain way and how the person should begin to think and act, the struggling Christian will continue to struggle.

When Christians go to counselors who are long on empathy, but short on biblical direction and correction, they initially may come away from their counseling sessions feeling good, motivated to deal with their problems. However, if the root issues are not addressed, possibly including sinful thoughts and behavior, and spiritual counsel is not given, then the good feelings fade and the motivation wanes for change. One in this situation can go for counseling indefinitely and yet find that significant healing and restoration continue to elude one.

It is a problem when Christian counselors address emotions but fail to give spiritual direction. It is also a problem when counselors give spiritual direction before the client is emotionally motivated to listen.

Sometimes motivation is not a problem. When the counselor senses from the very beginning that he or she has the trust of the counselee and discerns that the person is open for change, a lot of empathy and addressing of emotional issues is not necessary. Jay Adams gives a clear example of just such a person:

Millie, a Christian, had been in and out of mental institutions for thirteen years. No one seemed to be able to help her. She was lying around the house unable to do her housework, not caring for her children. Her husband was in complete despair and Millie, herself, was totally depressed. She was brought for counseling by friends from another state.

Millie's first visit made a remarkable change in her life. When a nouthetic counselor confronted her strongly on that first day about her lazy, undisciplined, irresponsible behavior and told her to go back to church, to get to work at home, to do her ironing and cleaning, everyone was shocked. That is, everyone but Millie, who responded with hope. Her husband was dumbfounded. Millie had been coddled by a psychiatrist for nearly a year. The psychiatrist listened to her sympathetically and sold her tranquilizers, yet there was no improvement.

After her first week of nouthetic counseling, on her own Millie laid her pills aside. She cleaned her house from stem to stern. When she returned the next week, she was driving the car herself, and she was a new woman. She had gone to church for the first time in years, to the amazement of the pastor and congregation. In just a few weeks, Millie was released from counseling. Several other problems, notably one with a son, were also solved during counseling. Counseling need not take long if one can lay his finger on the heart of the issue early, and if there is proper motivation on the part of the client.[4]

If there is "proper motivation on the part of the client," counseling can proceed without appealing to the emotions. If this is not the case, however, the counselor should follow the example God gives in Jonah chapter four.

God's Word tells that Jonah was very angry that God mercifully spared Nineveh from total destruction (4:1–2). In fact, he was so angry that he wanted to die (4:3). Rather than immediately rebuking him for a wrong feeling and an equally wrong desire, God addressed his emotion, "Do you have good reason to be angry?" Jonah did not respond, so God gave him an object lesson involving a shade plant and a worm. When the worm killed his shade plant, Jonah again wished to die (4:5–8). At this point, God again addressed Jonah's feelings of anger and said, "Do you have good reason to be angry about the plant?" Jonah replied, "I have good reason to be angry, even to death" (4:9). God then touched an emotional nerve in Jonah. He pointed out that Jonah cared more about a plant than thousands of people, many of whom did not know right from wrong (4:10–11). God knew that if He made contact with Jonah on an emotional level, Jonah would be open to spiritual direction.

If you have gone for counseling but have never felt understood or accepted by the counselor, perhaps he or she failed to connect with you on an emotional level. As a result, you may not trust his or her counsel, and counseling with that individual likely will not do you much good.

If you have received counsel from someone who understands and cares about you, but the good feelings you have in the office quickly disappear after you leave, then you are not getting sound, spiritual direction. You can go to this person for years and you probably will never make much progress in dealing with your problems.

In either of these cases, you need to look for a counselor who deals with people on both an emotional and spiritual level. A counselor who does so has the best chance of truly helping you.

Soul or spirit or both

Among many Christian counseling professionals there is an erroneous distinction made between people's emotional and spiritual makeup. Many Christian counselors view the *spirit* as completely distinct from the *soul*. Therefore, they conclude that psychologists and psychiatrists deal with emotions, while pastors and theologians address matters of the spirit.

The problem with this way of thinking is that the Bible does not clearly distinguish between the spirit and the soul. Although there is a distinction made between the two, there is an important overlap as well. As Charles Ryrie states, "Soul and spirit can relate to the same activities or emotions."[5]

There is no such thing as a human problem that is exclusively emotional or completely spiritual. The way one feels has an effect on one's thinking and behavior, and the way one thinks and behaves largely determines how one will feel. An effective counselor will be able to address both the emotions and the spirit. If only the emotional aspect of the problem is addressed, the struggling Christian will temporarily feel better, but these feelings won't last and the root problem will remain. If the counselor attempts to deal with only the spiritual dimension, without addressing the emotional, the struggling Christian will learn what to do about the problem but may be unmotivated to do it. Both emotional and spiritual aspects are important.

Summary

Unfortunately, there are many counselors today who are trained to help people emotionally, but not spiritually. In order to provide real spiritual direction and help, a counselor must know God's Word, put a priority on it, and be able to apply it in people's lives. But many counselors do not have a thorough knowledge of Scripture because they do not understand or they do not believe that the Bible is sufficient to address all spiritual/emotional problems a person may have. In chapter 4 we will examine why this is true.

Questions for Reflection and Action

1. Do you believe that your counselor understands how you feel and cares about you personally? If not, have you shared this with him or her?

2. Does your counselor primarily discuss your feelings or does he or she only address how you should act and think?

3. Do you come away from your counseling sessions with just good feelings or do you also come away with a better understanding of the spiritual issues involved in your situation and with biblical directions to deal with these issues?

Notes

[1]Frank Minirth and Walter Byrd, *Christian Psychiatry*. Old Tappan, NJ: Revell, 1990, p. 202.

[2]This is true when believers "quench the Spirit" (1 Thess. 5:19).

[3]Gary Collins, *Case Studies in Christian Counseling*. Waco, TX: Word, 1988, p. 81.

[4]Jay Adams, *Competent to Counsel*. Grand Rapids, MI: Zondervan, 1986, p. 141–2.

[5]Charles Ryrie, *Basic Theology*. Wheaton, IL: Victor, 1986, p. 197.

4. The Sufficiency of Scripture in Counseling

THE teenage boy slowly walked into my office and slouched down in a chair. He was angry, rebellious, withdrawn, and quite possibly suicidal. His parents had asked me to evaluate him and decide whether or not he was, in fact, suicidal. For two hours I encouraged him to talk about his feelings and circumstances as I carefully evaluated his emotional state. When my session with the boy was ended, I met with his parents and told them that I did not believe that he was likely to commit suicide, even though he was clearly struggling in a number of areas. I also informed them that I would be willing to counsel with him on a regular basis.

The couple listened attentively to what I had to say, thanked me for all my help, and then announced that they would be sending the youth to a psychologist in Iowa City. I was a little surprised, but not shocked. They had told me beforehand that they were considering just such a move. After they left my office, I put the whole situation behind me, until two weeks later, when I ran into the boy's mother at a local mall. The woman was very friendly and thanked me again for meeting with her son. Then she explained in a hushed tone that it really wasn't her idea to send their son to a psychologist. In practically a whisper she went on to tell me that her husband wanted someone "who uses more than just the Bible" to counsel their boy.

This man is not alone in his conviction that the Bible is insufficient for counseling. Many Christians and Christian counselors share his belief. So is the Bible enough? A well-known Christian psychologist has concluded:

> The Word of God never claims to have all the answers to all of life's problems. The Bible speaks to human needs today. It always will. But God in His goodness also has allowed us to discover psychological truths about human behavior and counseling that are never mentioned in Scripture, but are consistent with the written Word of God and helpful to people facing the problems of modern living.[1]

There are some important issues raised in this statement. First, what exactly does the Scripture claim for itself in regard to counseling? Although there is no verse in the Bible that explicitly answers this question, 2 Timothy 3:16 provides a satisfactory answer:

> All Scripture is inspired by God and profitable for teaching, for reproof, for correction, for training in righteousness; . . .

These words given to the apostle Paul by the Holy Spirit indicate that the Bible alone is enough to bring about instruction and correction that is truly life-changing. The word *teaching* refers to instruction about what a person should think and believe. *Reproof,* on the other hand, has to do with rebuking the errors in one's thinking and beliefs.[2] *Correction* refers to improving or restoring a person's behavior or conduct. And the other side of this is indicated by the phrase "training in righteousness," which means to instruct someone about how to act or behave.[3] God's Word provides everything people need for effecting positive changes in their mind and will. In addition, the Scripture provides what the counselor requires to effect positive change in a person's behavior. This is made clear by 2 Timothy 3:17:

> . . . that the man of God may be adequate, equipped for
> every good work.

The term *adequate* seems to indicate that God's Word is simply okay or just enough. But in fact, this word means "complete, proficient, able to meet all demands."[4] This is reinforced by the word *equipped* which means "fully supplied."[5] Everything we need to overcome problems in our thinking or behavior is in the Bible. It's all there.

We should note that 2 Timothy 3:16 does not address the issue of helping people to change their feelings. The Bible rarely commands us to feel a certain way or change the way we feel. The reason, as we discussed in the last chapter, is that our thoughts and behavior normally determine the way we feel. In other words, "You don't feel your way to good behavior, you behave your way into good feelings."[6]

This is why, for instance, the Bible tells husbands to love their wives (Eph. 5:25). This is not a command to feel love toward one's wife. Rather, as the context indicates, it is a command for husbands to behave properly toward their wives. Husbands are to "nourish" and "cherish" their wives (Eph. 5:28–29). These words refer to the husband's responsibility to provide physical and emotional security for his wife, and as a by-product, if a husband does this, his feelings of love for her will develop and grow.

Right thinking and behavior will lead to right feelings and emotions, and the Bible claims to provide everything that the counselor needs to address right thoughts and conduct. Now this does not mean that the Bible specifically addresses every human problem nor does it always give a specific answer to the problems that it does address. In *Can You Trust Psychology?* Gary Collins says,

> Some human problems are not mentioned in the Scripture. They are not discussed specifically, and neither are there examples to show how others dealt with these issues in a way pleasing to God.[7]

While this is true, we should not conclude that the Bible fails to give counselors all the help they need to address any of life's problems. Christian psychologist Larry Crabb asserts that

> the Bible is sufficient, because it provides either direct information or authoritative categories for answering all questions about how life should be lived on this earth and about how it can be lived according to an effective pattern. Whenever the Bible is not explicit about a given concern, biblical categories provide a framework for thinking through an adequate response to that concern.[8]

Even though the Bible does not address or illustrate all the specific problems and solutions we need for proper counseling, there are principles or categories in Scripture that guide us when resolving every specific problem.

What benefit then, if any, does psychology and other related disciplines have in Christian counseling? John Mac-Arthur, in his book *The Sufficiency of Christ,* responds to this question well when he says,

> Am I writing off every source of extrabiblical help as ut-
> terly worthless? Are there NO beneficial insights to be
> gained by looking at the observations of sociologists
> and psychologists?. . . Useful, perhaps. Necessary, no.
> If they are necessary, they are in Scripture. Otherwise,
> God has left us short of what we need, and that would
> be unthinkable.[9]

There are psychological techniques and truths "discovered" outside of the Bible. But these truths may be in Scripture in a more basic form or they may be expressed in different terms. The fact that much "extrabiblical truth" is actually in Scripture is acknowledged by professionals like William Kirwan, a Christian psychologist who admits that

> even though the Bible is not a psychology textbook, it
> informs us how we came to be the complicated emo-
> tional persons we are. In fact, the Bible's teachings con-
> tain in embryonic (and sometimes more fully
> developed) form all the valid teachings of modern be-
> havioral science.[10]

The bottom line is that psychology and other disciplines may either discover truth that is useful to the counseling process or rediscover truth that was already in Scripture. Regardless, the Bible contains all the truth that is essential to effective counseling. God's Word does have all the answers that are absolutely necessary, either specifically or in general principles.

But what about those who need "therapy"? What about people whose lives have been devastated by sexual abuse or torn apart by an ugly divorce? What about those who need healing for their broken lives? Can the Bible provide what is necessary for those hurting people? The answer is emphatically yes! In Psalm 19:7, David writes: "The law of the Lord is perfect, restoring the soul . . . ."

The word *perfect* means complete or whole.[11] The Bible is complete and whole, and it deals with everything necessary for us to be whole and complete again. The word *restoring* indicates this. As one understands and obeys God's Word, the person who is broken will be turned back or restored to wholeness.[12] This is not a superficial or surface restoration, but a restoration that affects the very core of one's being.

The word *soul* can simply be used as another word for "person." However, some believe that in this context the word refers to the inner person,[13] the actual "soul" of a person, and I believe that is the correct understanding. When people accept and act on God's Word, profound inner change begins to take place. Change may not take place overnight or dramatically, but restoration can take place no matter how broken or confused a person's life has become.

Author and teacher Neil Anderson tells a true story of a Christian woman who had been severely depressed for years. As he puts it, "She survived by leaning on friends, three counseling sessions a week, and a variety of prescription drugs." But she came to one of his seminars where he spoke about the believer's identity in Christ. The depressed woman realized during the conference that she had not been depending on God or His Word for her help. She went home and began trusting daily in Christ and His Word alone for help with her depression. Everything else was set aside. In one month she went from being a "broken" woman to being a "whole" person.[14] Restoration does not always come this quickly. In fact, it usually does not. Restoration is often a long process. But the point is that God's Word can make it happen!

Larry Crabb affirms this truth when he says,

> I accept a distinction between counseling and therapy, but I insist that the Bible is both essential and sufficient, not only for "counseling" in general, but also for that specific form of counseling which is commonly labeled "therapy."
>
> In my understanding, the Bible teaches principles that can comprehensively guide our efforts to counsel with warmth and insight, and it lays out truths about human personality that are sufficient for leading us into a thorough understanding of what therapists call "dynamics."
>
> When I argue for biblical sufficiency, I am suggesting that every question a counselor or therapist needs to ask is answered by both the content of Scripture and its implications.[15]

Summary

The Bible claims to deal with everything that is needed to effect positive change in thought and behavior. And if we think and act properly, we will feel right as well.

The Bible does not mention every human problem specifically, nor does it give all the specific answers we may need. However, the Bible does give principles from which specific answers can be gleaned by a wise counselor. This is why counselors are so important. Counselors who know God's Word and are able to accurately pull out principles and apply them to people's lives are very much needed today. True, it is the Spirit of God who guides us into all truth (John 16:13), but God has chosen to use wise counselors in the process (Prov. 11:14).

In spite of what the Bible claims for itself, some Christians still have a problem with the concept of Scripture being sufficient for counseling. There are people, I am sure, reading this book who would say from past experience, "I've been to a Christian counselor who claims to believe the Bible and I'm still not better. What went wrong?" If the Bible is in fact sufficient for all our needs, then why do so many people feel unhelped by Christian counselors? Chapter 5 will show how counselors sometimes use the Bible effectively and sometimes fail to appropriate the wisdom and power of Scripture.

For more help

For further reading and study regarding the sufficiency of Scripture for counseling, I recommend Larry Crabb's book *Understanding People.* Crabb has a Ph.D. in psychology, yet he convincingly argues for the sufficiency of Scripture in regard to counseling. See chapters 1–4 in particular for his specific reasons and explanations.

Notes

[1]Gary Collins, *Can You Trust Psychology?* Downers Grove, IL: InterVarsity Press, 1988, p. 97.

[2]W. Bauer, W. F. Arndt, F. W. Gingrich, *Greek-English Lexicon.* Chicago, IL: U of Chicago Press, 1957, p. 269.

[3]See George W. Knight, *Commentary on the Pastoral Epistles.* Grand Rapids, MI: Eerdman's, 1992, pp. 449–50; and John R.W. Stott, *The Message of II Timothy.* Downers Grove, IL: InterVarsity Press, 1973, p. 103.

[4]W. Bauer, W. F. Arndt, F. W. Gingrich, p. 501.

[5]Fritz Rienecker, *A Linguistic Key to the Greek New Testament, Vol. 2.* Grand Rapids, MI: Zondervan, 1980, p. 301.

[6]Neil Anderson, *Victory Over the Darkness.* Ventura, CA: Regal, 1990, p. 32.

[7]Gary Collins, p. 95.

[8]Larry Crabb, *Understanding People.* Grand Rapids, MI: Zondervan, 1987, p. 47.

[9]John MacArthur, *Our Sufficiency In Christ.* Waco, TX: Word, 1991, p. 121.

[10]William Kirwan, *Biblical Concepts for Christian Counseling.* Grand Rapids, MI: Baker, 1984, p. 73.

[11]Francis Brown, S. R. Driver, C. A Briggs, *Hebrew and English Lexicon of the Old Testament..* Oxford, England: Clarendon Press, 1975, p. 1071.

[12]Ibid., p. 996.

[13]Ibid., p. 661.

[14]Neil Anderson, pp. 11–12.

[15]Larry Crabb, p. 62.

5. The Use of Scripture in Counseling

N OT long ago I counseled a believer who was having major emotional problems. He was struggling with both depression and anxiety and it had rendered him almost totally dysfunctional. As I talked with him extensively and evaluated his situation, it was clear to me that his basic problem was spiritual. When I shared my conclusion with him he did not disagree. He admitted that his root problem was a lack of faith, and he knew that he was going to have to trust God a lot more in order to get better. After we discussed at length what the Bible indicated he should do, both of us agreed on a biblical plan of action. I was convinced that we were on the right track, but too much was at stake for me to simply rest on my evaluation.

It was clear that he would also require medical treatment, so I referred him to a Christian psychiatrist at a well-known clinic for an independent evaluation. I assumed that since I was sending my client to a Christian clinic he would be evaluated by a Christian psychiatrist. But, to my surprise, that was not the case. Instead, he was referred to a secular psychologist who evaluated him with a standard battery of psychological tests. The evaluation had nothing to do with Scripture, and it did not address the spiritual issues involved in his life.

He was finally put under the care of a Christian therapist who also evaluated him. The therapist told my client that his primary problem was that his parents did not sufficiently express their love for him when he was a child. In order for him to get better, he was told to meet weekly with a secular therapist, a secular co-dependency support group, and a secular addiction support group, as well as with me.

If you are a struggling believer, you may have gone to a Christian counselor or clinic. You may have assumed, as I did, that the evaluation and proposed treatment would be ultimately based on Scripture, even if it was not explicitly so. But as the example I related indicates, just because a counselor or clinic is "Christian" does not mean that the Bible plays a major role in evaluation and treatment.

In his book *Can You Trust Psychology?*, Gary Collins makes this revealing statement:

> There is no way to prove it. It's only a hunch. I hope it isn't true. But my conversations with Christian counselors over the years have left me with the uncomfortable impression that most of them don't counsel in ways much different from those of their secular colleagues.[1]

This is a very disturbing disclosure by a prominent Christian counselor. What he is saying is that he believes that "most" Christian counselors do not counsel people in a way that is uniquely Christian, and from my experience I would have to agree with him. The question then is, where have Christian counselors gotten off track?

The answer can be found in the following comment by Larry Crabb in *Understanding People:*

> In my view, many Christian counselors have adopted a method of study that treats the Bible as helpful, informative, and insightful—but neither authoritative nor sufficient. As a result the Bible is weakened. No longer is Scripture permitted to speak with a final word. We rarely turn to its pages for answers to certain kinds of personal questions. Psychology has usurped the place of the Bible in the minds of many who would strongly argue for revelation as the necessary route to knowledge.[2]

In other words, many Christian counselors say that God's Word is their final authority, and that there is much within its pages that is helpful for counseling. However, in reality, these Christian counselors use the Bible and biblical principles sparingly, and because of this approach to counseling, the Bible does not end up being the "final word."

These counselors would undoubtedly disagree with this assessment. They believe that they are using Scripture effectively and allowing it to be their final authority. Read the words of Collins:

> All truths discovered by human beings must be tested against and proved consistent with the revealed Word of God. If the Bible is true, we cannot have psychological discoveries that are also true but inconsistent with the Scriptures. The Christian scholar tests his or her findings against the Scripture; we do not try to vali-

date the Scriptures by testing them against knowledge discovered by human endeavor. To state this more specifically: the Christian tests psychology against the Bible, not the Bible against psychology.[3]

But the problem with this method is that it still tends, in practice, to water down the authority of Scripture and to render the Bible merely "helpful." As Crabb says,

> Notice where this reasoning leads. Our efforts to understand counseling do not need to be guided by the Bible; we must only make sure that whatever conclusions we reach are consistent with the Bible. The difference between "guided by" and "consistent with" is enormous. The theorist who is guided by the Bible more fully acknowledges its authority. Someone who depends for guidance on another source and then seeks to maintain biblical consistency will tend to regard the Bible merely as helpful.[4]

This is why many Christian counselors give direction and counsel to people that, when followed, does not help or does not continue to help. The reason is that these counselors rely on psychology and extra-biblical sources of truth first and foremost, rather than on God's Word. But why is this the case?

I believe that the majority of these counselors are well-intentioned Christian people. The problem is that most of them do not know the Bible well. They usually do not have an adequate working knowledge of Scripture nor do they understand how to adequately interpret and apply it. Therefore, they lean on their primary training and knowledge, which is normally in the areas of psychology and counseling techniques. People naturally rely on that which they know best and in which they have their most training. For many Christian counselors that is not the Bible, it is psychology. If these counselors knew God's Word better, they would have greater confidence in it and would rely on it more. This is why I maintain the conviction that anyone who desires to counsel needs to have extensive training in Scripture and how to interpret it. And this training should come first, as the foundation for all that may follow. I am not willing to say that any kind of education or training beyond a biblical education is wrong or superfluous. But it is a supplement, however important, to that which is basic and absolutely essential.

When a struggling believer goes to a Christian counselor who gives psychological evaluations and treatment plans, but fails to give biblical direction and counsel, that person will continue to struggle, and the counselee will grow disenchanted and frustrated because real healing and growth is not taking place.

When a hurting Christian goes to a counselor and receives counsel that seems biblical and seems to work, he or she is going to be satisfied and encouraged for a while. But if the counsel given is not truly biblical, it will not continue to work and the counselee will then be more confused and hurt than ever. And this is exactly where many Christians are today. But it is not because the Bible is insufficient. It is because many Christian counselors rely primarily or exclusively on secular resources, rather than on God's Word.

Why isn't it working?

At this point someone may be saying, "I went to a counselor who actually referred to the Bible and used Bible verses as the basis for counsel. Why didn't it help me?"

There are two primary reasons why biblical counsel is not always effective, and neither one has anything to do with Scripture's being insufficient for counseling. Rather, these reasons relate to motivation and application.

In Colossians 1:28, Paul says,

> We proclaim Him, admonishing every man and teach-
> ing every man with all wisdom, that we may present ev-
> ery man complete in Christ.

In order to counsel people to completeness or maturity in Christ, counselors have to be willing to "admonish." This word means "to exert influence upon the will and decisions of another with the object of guiding him or her into a generally accepted code of behavior or of encouraging him or her to observe certain instructions."[5]

"Biblical" counselors like Jay Adams rightly recognize the importance of "admonishing" people in counseling. In fact, Adams has constructed an entire counseling methodology based on this word.[6] Counselors like Adams often refer to Colossians 1:28 as the key passage in Scripture affirming their counseling methodology.[7] However, there is clearly more to counseling than simply "admonishing." To help people become "complete in Christ," a counselor has to be involved in "teaching every man with all wisdom" as well. But what is it that counselees need to be taught?

Christians who are struggling with emotional/spiritual problems often need to understand, first of all, why they have their problems, and secondly, why they are not getting better. These two steps are often needed to provide proper motivation to follow a biblical course of action.

Some counselors, like Adams, say that

> all the *why* that a counselee needs to know can be clearly
> demonstrated in the *what*. What was done? What must
> be done to rectify it? What should future responses be?
> In nouthetic counseling the stress falls upon the "what"
> rather than the "why" because the why is already known

before counseling begins. The reason why people get in trouble in their relationships to God and others is because of their sinful natures. Men are born sinners.[8]

The sinfulness of men and women certainly explains some of the problems that Christians have. Christians still retain our sinful nature, and believers do sin (1 John 1:8–10). Also, personal sin is involved in problems that people regularly bring to counselors. Nevertheless, the fact that Christians sin and have a sin nature does not explain every situation. Some questions still remain. Why do Christians who are indwelt and led by the Holy Spirit choose to sin by following the leading of the world, the flesh, and the devil rather than God?[9] An even tougher question is why did Adam and Eve sin? They were not created with a sin nature, and until the time they disobeyed God, they had never sinned. What happened?

The Bible does not tell us explicitly what happened, but it is clear from a careful study of the creation account what occurred.

In the beginning, God made man and woman in His image and put them both in charge of all His creation (Gen. 1:26). He also placed them in a beautiful garden to take care of it (Gen. 2:15). Why did He do this? Was it simply to accomplish His divine purposes, or was it to provide for needs that He had created in man and woman? I believe that God had both of these purposes in mind.

In *The Hunger for Significance,* R. C. Sproul stays that

every person needs to feel significant. We want our lives to count. We yearn to believe that in some way we are important. And that hunger for significance—a drive as intense as our need for oxygen—does not come from pride or ego. It comes from God . . . .[10]

God has created in each of us a basic need for significance. We need to feel that our lives have meaning and purpose, and God has met that need by giving us important status and labor to do.

In a similar way, God created men and women with a basic need for love and acceptance. People need to know that someone really cares about them and accepts them for who they are. God met this need by giving Adam a wife (Gen. 2:25), and by spending time with them Himself (Gen. 3:8).

Even though our need for love and significance can be met in part through human means and relationships, these needs can never be fully met without a continuing, personal relationship with God. Deep down, people thirst for the true and living God, and only He can truly satisfy our most basic needs (Psalm 42:1–2; Psalm 63:1). Nevertheless, people try to meet these legitimate needs through illegitimate or sinful means. In fact, this occurred back at the very beginning.

In the Garden of Eden, God was meeting every need that Adam and Eve had: physical, spiritual, and emotional. He provided food, meaningful labor, fellowship with Himself. There was no good reason for man and woman to look elsewhere. But unfortunately, Eve was deceived by Satan (Gen. 3:13), and then Adam sinned knowingly (1 Tim. 2:14).

Why Adam and Eve responded sinfully to Satan's deceptive words we ultimately cannot say. We face the same dilemma in ascertaining why Satan would rebel against God when He was experiencing all the wonder and blessing of God's presence. Obviously, the problem was not that Adam and Eve were inherently sinful. They had never sinned before and they were not created with a propensity to sin. God pronounced man and woman as well as the rest of creation "good" (Gen. 1:31).

Whatever the ultimate reason (and only God knows), Adam and Eve turned to sinful means to satisfy their deepest human needs. In doing so, they plunged the whole human race into sin and established a sinful pattern of meeting legitimate human needs in illegitimate ways. People have followed their lead ever since.

The matter of motivation

When Christians attempt to satisfy their need for love and significance through sinful means, they will inevitably fail. If these needy Christians then go for counseling and the counselor simply points out their sin and admonishes them to do what is biblically correct, they might respond appropriately to this counsel. Then again they might not, because they are not sufficiently motivated to do it. It is true that the Spirit leads us toward what is right (Rom. 8:14), but He does not force or irresistibly cause us to do what is right. Christians can and do quench the Spirit (1 Thess. 5:19).

In some counseling situations, the counselor must teach the counselee about the needs he or she is trying to meet through sinful means, and then point out that one's needs can only be met through a close relationship with God and by following His instructions. When the counselee understands this he or she will often be motivated to immediately begin doing what is right, and if not, one at least understands why one's present course of action is futile, and the Spirit can use this truth to eventually bring one to a point of acceptance.

Human helpers

Now some may say that if the counselor brings up the issue of human need, this simply gives the counselee an excuse. The troubled person can use one's needs as an excuse for one's problems and one's conduct rather than face squarely one's personal responsibility.

But human need can only be used as an excuse if the counselor allows it to be used as such. The counselee does have certain needs, but one has a choice about how one will meet those needs. On the other hand, if one takes the position that people, including Christians, are simply sinful, a counselee can always say, "I'm just a sinner; what else can you expect?"

The truth is that if one wants to excuse one's behavior or blame one's problems on others, one can always find some way to do it. But Christian counselors must always insist that believers have a choice. Christians can either attempt to meet their God-given human needs through purely human, sinful means, or they can reach out to God and follow His prescriptions. The choice is always there. Sometimes the counselee does decide to follow God and do what the Bible says, and yet doesn't know exactly what he or she should do. This is why the Christian counselor must also teach "with all wisdom" (Col. 1:28). Knowledge is not wisdom. Wisdom includes knowledge, but it is more than that. It is the ability to apply knowledge skillfully to real life situations.

Counselors have to realize that even though believers know what Scripture says and want to obey it, he or she may not know how. Proverbs 11:14 says that "where there is no guidance, the people fall, but in the abundance of counselors there is victory." The Bible is clear that wise, human counselors are needed in order to give guidance to people who will otherwise fall. The question then is, what kind of guidance is Proverbs 11:14 referring to? Is it some kind of human wisdom unrelated to Scripture, or is it the practical application of Scripture to everyday life? I believe it is the latter.

The Bible is sufficient for every counseling situation in that it provides all the basic information necessary to effectively help people. However, wise counselors will often be needed to draw out the principles from God's Word and then aid in the application of those biblical principles.

To accomplish this task, the counselor has to have a thorough knowledge of God's Word. This is the number one prerequisite for effective counseling. Without a good working knowledge of the Bible, the counselor cannot hope to help hurting people.

Some time ago my wife was listening to a Christian radio station when a woman who is a Christian leader and author was taking calls from people who wanted advice and counsel. A call came from a young pastor's wife, a mother with a dilemma. Apparently her husband was, in her opinion, overly dedicated to his congregation and therefore did not want to leave the church at Christmas. The woman who called deeply longed to fly home with her young child to be with family at Christmas. No doubt this woman was feeling neglected by her husband who appeared to care more for his congregation than for her and their young family.

This was the woman's counsel to this wife. She told her to buy plane tickets for herself and her child to fly for Christmas and to tell her husband that if he wanted to stay with the church members, he could, but she was going home regardless.

This "counsel" is not biblical wisdom. This type of counsel will not only fail to help struggling people, it could very easily make their problems worse. The importance of giving counsel that is truly biblical cannot be overstated.

In addition to this, the effective counselor has to either have the innate or learned ability to put biblical knowledge into principles. Counselors must help counselees draw principles for life and healing from the Bible, and then help them apply these biblical principles specifically to their lives. This is where real life experience comes into play and is so vitally important.

Anyone who knows the Bible well and can explain it in general principles is competent to teach God's Word. But to effectively counsel married couples, for example, the counselor needs to bring practical experience in applying scriptural principles to marital relationships. It is one thing for an unmarried pastor to preach what God's Word says about marriage in terms of general principles. It is another thing altogether for him to counsel people with troubled marriages. That is not to say that he cannot do it at all, but to be most effective, the wise counselor needs to have practical, personal experience in applying God's Word.

In marital counseling I regularly work with husbands who know that the Bible commands them to "love your wives, just as Christ also loved the church and gave Himself up for her" (Eph. 5:25). Unfortunately, some of these men do not know specifically how to do this. They know that this means they should not beat their wives or come home drunk every night. But these men do not know more specifically what they *should* do. In some cases these men grew up in homes where they did not have fathers who taught them by word and example how to love a wife. They know generally what to do, and they want to obey God, but someone has to teach them "with all wisdom" how to apply Ephesians 5:25 in their marriages.

I remember very well a Christian man who came to see me several years ago. His wife was on the verge of leaving him. She was so frustrated and unhappy with the relationship that she was beside herself. He knew things were not good at home, but he could not figure out what the big fuss was all about. After all, he told me, he provided very well for his wife financially and he was never unfaithful to her. I asked him how often he verbally told his wife he loved her. He replied, "At least two, maybe even three times a year!" I almost burst out laughing, but then I realized from the expression on his face that the man was not joking. He sincerely thought he was doing a good and acceptable job of expressing his love for his wife. And he went on to explain that, to the best of his knowledge, his father never told his mother that he loved her!

During the course of the next year, I counseled with this man who genuinely wanted to obey Ephesians 5:25. We got very specific in applying this verse to his life, and we even sought some input from his wife. He learned how to love his wife well. So well that they now have a very good and happy relationship.

Summary

Biblical counseling is often effective because it is based on God's Word, as opposed to counseling that is largely based on psychology or other human wisdom. Nevertheless, many Christians who go to biblical counselors are not getting all the help they need. These believers require more than admonishing. In many cases these struggling Christians need to be taught what legitimate human needs they have and why sinful means will never bring satisfaction or healing.

In addition, these struggling believers require help in applying God's Word to their lives. A general exhortation and plan will not suffice. Specific and wise counsel will be necessary. Counselors must follow through on everything that Colossians 1:28 teaches in order for every man [and woman] to be "complete in Christ."

Questions for reflection and action

1. Does your counselor acknowledge Scripture as the final authority in regard to all that is true? If you are not sure, ask.
2. Do you think that the counseling you are receiving is biblical or human wisdom?
3. Does your counselor believe that one begins in counseling with biblical data and then supplements this with natural or scientific discoveries or that one begins with natural and scientific data and then it is tested against biblical revelation? If you don't know, talk with him or her about this important matter.
4. Does your counselor simply quote Scripture to you or give you general biblical principles or does he or she also help you to specifically apply God's Word to your life situation?

5. Does your counselor attempt to point out from Scripture what is motivating you or does he or she simply tell you what is biblically wrong and exhort you to do what is biblically right?

Notes

[1]Gary Collins, *Can You Trust Psychology?* Downers Grove, IL: InterVarsity Press, 1988, p. 51.

[2]Larry Crabb, *Understanding People.* Grand Rapids, MI: Zondervan, 1987, p. 37.

[3]Gary Collins, pp. 94–95.

[4]Larry Crabb, p. 39.

[5]Colin Brown, ed., *New International Dictionary of New Testament Theology.* Grand Rapids, MI: Zondervan, 1975, p. 567.

[6]Jay Adams, *Competent to Counsel.* Grand Rapids, MI: Zondervan, 1986, p. 41–64.

[7]Ibid., p. 42.

[8]Ibid., p. 48.

[9]See the author's book, *Why Christians Sin,* for a full discussion of this question.

[10]R. C. Sproul, *The Hunger for Significance.* Ventura, CA: Gospel Light, 1991, book jacket.

6. Spiritual Warfare

Y EARS ago when I was just beginning pastoral ministry a very disturbed woman began attending our church. This woman was extremely angry about her lot in life, in particular, the husband she felt stuck with. She was also clinically depressed. I never saw her smile or laugh; her face was always expressionless. I counseled with her on a number of occasions and tried to encourage her to see a Christian psychiatrist, which I believe she did. But neither my efforts nor anyone else's seemed to have any effect on her. Then one day she unexpectedly burst into my office. She was radiant! She was smiling from ear to ear. At first I was eager to learn what had changed, but after she told me what had transpired, I was reluctant to accept her explanation.

The woman explained that she had been under tremendous demonic oppression for some time and that the previous night she had been released from Satan's bondage. She said her problems were now behind her, and she was praising God for her deliverance.

As she relayed all this to me the woman could tell I was skeptical. I did not share her enthusiasm because I had little confidence in this so-called "deliverance." My response disappointed her a little, but I think she expected it. As she left, she encouraged me not to simply dismiss her account of what had happened to her—but I did.

While I fully expected her to lapse back into depression in the days and weeks that followed, she never did. Finally she landed a job and moved with her family to another part of the city, and I never saw her again.

As I reflect on this incident, I realize that I was like a lot of pastors and Christian counselors today. I believed that Satan is a real person and that he is waging war against God and His people. I also believed that Satan has deployed thousands of fallen angels to do his bidding and wreak havoc in this world. I did not believe, however, that Satan and his demons could be a serious threat to genuine believers, nor did I believe that satanic attacks were a common occurrence. I underestimated Satan's power and influence and assumed that when a believer was having problems they were due to sin, emotional trauma, or physical problems. I was wrong, and so are many pastors and counselors today who still view Satan as a minor or infrequent foe.

In Ephesians 6:12 Paul tells us that "our struggle is not against flesh and blood, but against the rulers, against the powers, against the world-forces of this darkness, against the spiritual forces of wickedness in the heavenly places."

In this passage we see, first of all, that when Christians struggle, Satan is involved to a great extent. The battle is not ultimately between us and someone else made of flesh and blood. It may appear that one's struggle is with a spouse, a boss, the children, or some other person. But God's Word says that the real battle is a spiritual one between us and the powers of darkness. What's more, this is a fierce spiritual battle.

The word *struggle* here refers to hand-to-hand combat where any means of inflicting a wound is acceptable, or to a wrestling match where all the rules of fair play have been tossed out.[1] Satan has no intention of playing fair. He cannot have us once we have trusted Christ. He cannot tear us out of God's powerful hand (John 10:28). However, he can do tremendous damage to us.

First Peter 5:8 says, "Be of sober spirit, be on the alert. Your adversary, the devil, prowls about like a roaring lion seeking someone to devour." Peter is not saying that Satan can literally "devour" us, nor is he implying that Satan has the power to separate us from God or take away our salvation (Rom. 8:31–39). But what he is indicating is that Satan can ruin our lives here on earth. He can make us miserable and render us ineffective for God. A tragic example of this fact is seen in the life of a women I counseled some time ago.

This dear woman had been miserable most of her life. She had a terrible childhood and marriage. She was sexually abused first by a relative and then by her husband. This is enough to cause anyone intense emotional pain. But Satan made matters worse by accusing her of bringing all this abuse on herself, and of being a complete failure as a wife and mother. Unfortunately, this hurting person believed these satanic messages and as a result, her severe emotional pain was increased by feelings of incredible guilt. What's more, Satan kept telling her that she was not really a child of God. She had virtually no assurance of salvation but instead was plagued by tremendous doubts. I asked her if she understood how a person is saved. Her ambiguous answer prompted me to explain the gospel to her. I then asked her if she wanted to make sure she was saved by praying to trust Christ as her Savior. She quickly said yes. When she was through asking God to save her because of what Jesus had done, she looked up at me and said, "I'm hearing that voice again." I asked what the voice was saying. She said, "You still belong to me and your prayer will not help you." At this point I told her that this voice was not the Holy Spirit. It was demonic. I then began to explain to her how she could be free of Satan's bondage and resist him daily. I believe she broke free that day and now has Satan on the run. Even though the battle continues, this woman is now beginning to win the struggle.

The problem today is that even if people understand that Satan is heavily involved in the struggles that Christians have, most believers and Christian counselors do not really know how to deal with him. There is a lot of confusion in the area of spiritual warfare. The truth is that we are never commanded in the New Testament to exorcise demons, rebuke or bind Satan, or rid believers of ancestral curses.[2] What the Bible does command us to do is to "resist" Satan by putting on the whole armor of God (Eph. 6:13).

In Ephesians 6:14–15, Paul begins to discuss the "armor of God":

> Stand firm therefore, having girded your loins with
> truth, and having put on the breastplate of righteous-
> ness, and having shod your feet with the preparation of
> the gospel of peace.

Each of these three pieces of protective armor relate to a proper understanding of the "truth," and in particular, what God has done for us through Christ Jesus. Neil Anderson says, "[Satan] knows that if he can keep you from understanding who you are in Christ, he can keep you from experiencing the maturity and freedom which is your inheritance as a child of God."[3] Anderson goes on to explain that

> no person can consistently behave in a way that is in-
> consistent with the way he perceives himself. If you

think you're a no-good bum, you'll probably live like a no-good bum. But if you see yourself as a child of God who is spiritually alive in Christ, you'll begin to live in victory and freedom as He lived. Next to a knowledge of God, a knowledge of who you are is by far the most important truth you can possess.[4]

In order to resist Satan and stand firm, Christians need to be "girded . . . with truth," which refers to a proper understanding of who God is and what He has done for us. In addition, we "put on the breastplate of righteousness" when we understand that God sees us as righteous in Christ (1 Cor. 1:30). Our primary identity in Jesus is that we are no longer sinners, but rather we are now saints (1 Cor. 1:2). In a similar way, our spiritual footing is stabilized when we recognize that as a result of accepting the "gospel of peace," we are no longer enemies of God, but rather we have been "reconciled to God through the death of His Son" (Rom. 5:10).

As a pastor I can testify to the fact that many Christians do not really know who they are in Christ. The Bible says much about who we are now in Christ and all of these truths are important for us to know if we are going to effectively resist Satan's attacks.[5] But it is not enough to simply know the truth, we must actively believe it and act on it.

Paul continues his discussion of the armor of God in Ephesians 6:16–17:

> . . . taking up the shield of faith with which you will be able to extinguish all the flaming missiles of the evil one. And take the helmet of salvation, and the sword of the Spirit, which is the word of God.

The "shield of faith" refers to the Christian's equipment for actively believing the truth and fighting off satanic accusations and lies with the truth.

In 2 Corinthians 10:5, Paul states that we are to be "taking every thought captive to the obedience of Christ." If Satan plants a thought in one's mind that is contrary to the obedience of Christ, one must not believe it or allow it to dwell in one's mind. Reject and extinguish it by believing the truth.

If, for instance, Satan tries to tell you that you are not really saved, you must not believe him, but "take the helmet of salvation" by believing what God's Word says about your future with God. God's Word is the sword of the Spirit. We need to know it and use it against Satan just as Christ did (Matt. 4:1–11).

The tremendous importance of knowing and believing God's Word in order to effectively resist Satan is painfully seen in Eve's encounter with him in Genesis 3:1–6. When Satan approached Eve he deliberately distorted God's command (3:1). He made it appear as if God were not being fair or reasonable. In other words, he questioned the goodness of God. Eve began to believe his lie about God, because in her reply to Satan she also distorted what God had said (3:2–3). When Satan saw that Eve did not completely believe the truth, he directly challenged God's Word (3:4) and was able to deceive her (3:5–6).

It is crucial that Christians put on the full armor of God and resist Satan by knowing and believing the truth. Otherwise, to the extent that we believe satanic lies and accusations, we are under his control. Now "demonic control does not mean satanic ownership."[6] Christians belong to God, and we will always belong to Him (Eph. 1:13–14). But whenever and to whatever extent we begin to believe Satan rather than God, we are to that extent controlled by Satan.

The New Testament passage that best indicates that believers can be controlled by Satan is Acts 5:1–5. In this account it is clear that Ananias and Sapphira both were believers. Only a Christian indwelt by the Spirit can "lie to the Holy Spirit" (5:4), and from the "great fear [that] came upon the whole church" when they were disciplined, it is apparent that Ananias and Sapphira were genuine members of it. Why they decided to listen to Satan and then, as a result, attempt to deceive the church about their gift, the Bible does not tell us (5:4). Whatever the reason, because they believed a satanic lie they came under his control. Control is what the word *filled* indicates (5:3). It is the same word used in Ephesians 5:18 where Paul commands us to "be filled with the Spirit." Just as we can decide to stop sinning and submit to God, and thus allow the Holy Spirit to control our lives, we can also be controlled by Satan if we believe and act on satanic lies and accusations.

If a believer struggling with demonic control goes to a counselor who does not believe that Satan can control believers, the client is not going to get much help. Discussion of either emotional issues or the need to stop sinning will not be enough to really help a Christian in this predicament. The reality of demonic control first must be recognized, and then the believer must be set free through knowing and believing the truth.

On the other hand, there are some counselors today who give the devil too much credit. I heard about just such a counselor a few years ago who diagnosed almost every client who came to him as being under demonic control. If a person was struggling with weight, the counselor said that he or she had the "demon of gluttony." If another individual was struggling with low self-esteem, he pronounced him or her as having the "demon of self-hatred." His remedy for every situation was exorcism. But people did not get better. The problem with this type of counseling and treatment (aside from the fact that we are not instructed in Scripture to do exorcisms) is that it denies personal responsibility on the part of the believer and it implies that Satan can cause Christians to sin. One counselor responds to this way of thinking when he says,

> I never tolerate someone saying, "The devil made me do it . . . ." No, he didn't make you do it, you did it. Somewhere along the line you chose to give the devil a foothold. He merely took advantage of the opportunity you gave him. You have all the resources and protection you need to live a victorious life in Christ every day. If you're not living it, it's your choice.[7]

Satan cannot cause us to sin. His control of the believer is never direct or total. First John 5:18 says, "We know that no one who is born of God sins; But He who was born of God keeps him, and the evil one does not touch him." This verse of Scripture indicates that a true Christian will not sin continuously.[8] But in addition, this passage indicates that Satan cannot force us to sin. The verb *touch* means "to take hold of."[9] Some interpret this to mean that Satan cannot harm us, at least not without God's permission. But the immediate context has to do with Christians sinning (5:16–18). Therefore, I believe that it is best to understand this verse as indicating that Satan can no longer lay hold of us to make us sin.

Before Christ, we were under Satan's control and power (Eph. 2:1–3). But we have been set free in Christ (Gal. 5:1) and therefore Satan only controls us indirectly when we believe and act on his lies rather than following the leading of the Spirit (Rom. 8:14).

When we decide to follow the Holy Spirit's leading, He provides us with all the power we need to do what is right. In a battle between the Spirit and Satan, the Holy Spirit will triumph every time (1 John 4:4). The major question is whether the Christian is going to believe God or believe Satan. This is also true in regard to the "flesh."

In Romans 7:15–20, Paul discusses the "flesh" and its powerful influence in his life as a Christian:

> That which I am doing, I do not understand; for I am not
> practicing what I would like to do, but I am doing the
> very thing I hate. But if I do the very thing I do not wish
> to do, I agree with the Law, confessing that it is good.
> So now, no longer am I the one doing it, but sin which
> indwells me. For I know that nothing good dwells in
> me, that is, in my flesh; for the wishing is present in me,
> but the doing of good is not. For the good that I wish, I
> do not do; but I practice the very evil that I do not wish.
> But if I am doing the very thing I do not wish, I am no
> longer the one doing it, but sin which dwells in me.

When Paul refers to the flesh in this passage he is not speaking of his physical body or existence, he is talking about "that anti-God, self-reliant aspect of all human beings . . . . That is the seat of sin, engaging in unremitting resistance to the Holy Spirit."[10] In other words, it is the source of sinful desires in the believer.

Many times during the course of a day, believers have to decide whether they are going to follow the Spirit's leading and do what is right, or give in to the sinful desires of the flesh and do what is wrong. The flesh is a powerful influence for evil, but the Spirit is a far more powerful influence for good. Ultimately the decision is ours to make. We can allow the Spirit to control us (Eph. 5:18) or we can decide to let Satan or the flesh control us (Rom. 6:12). There are other facts involved that influence our decision and many of them we have already discussed. But the bottom line is that believers regularly decide whether they will follow the Spirit or give in to the flesh.

There are some Christians who believe that this decision is not ultimately or always ours to make. One theologian states that "a Christian can become so weak, so spiritually undernourished, so ignorant that the flesh level of his personhood, which is supposed to be his slave, rises up to act as his master."[11]

But if the flesh can rise up and irresistibly cause the believer to sin even when he or she desires to do what is right, then logically the believer is not always responsible for his or her sin and one's ability to do what is right is severely hampered because he or she has no control over sin under certain circumstances.

It is better to understand Paul's words as indicating that the flesh is the *source* of sinful desires, not the *cause* of sinful acts. There was a sense in which Paul always desired to do what was right. That was the work of the Spirit in his life. The Holy Spirit not only gives believers the ability to do what is right, but at the same time He strongly urges us to do it. Even so, we must decide to obey the Spirit's leading and tap into His power.

This is why Paul commands believers in Galatians 5:16 to "walk by the Spirit." This means we should follow the Spirit's directions as we journey through life. If we do, Paul states that "we will not carry out the desire of the flesh." The word *not* in this verse is a "strong negative."[12] It can be translated "not at all." Even though we decide to follow the Spirit's leading, however, there is no doubt that we will sometimes sin. But if we give in to the flesh we will certainly sin.

William Lawrence states that "unless we understand the flesh and how it works in us we can never be free from sin . . . ignorance in this area of spiritual reality is deadly."[13] Once again, the Christian must not only know the truth, but also actively believe it in order to defeat Satan and the flesh in spiritual warfare.

If you are still struggling to make progress with your problems, even after extensive counseling or therapy, maybe you are losing the battle in spiritual warfare. Many counselors either do not think there is really a war going on or they do not understand how to properly fight it. The result is that a lot of Christians are spiritual casualties. That's the bad news. Perhaps you are one of them. The good news is that you do not have to continue under the control of either the flesh or the devil. When you understand and believe the truth of who God is and who you are in Christ you will be set free. Then the choice is truly yours either to go back to bondage and sin or live free!

But what if you've been emotionally traumatized? What if you are so broken that you can't do what is right? Chapter 7 will explore the answers to these important questions.

Notes

[1]Markus Barth, "Ephesians 4–6," *The Anchor Bible,* Vol. 34A. Garden City, NJ: Doubleday, 1974, p. 763.

[2]Thomas Ice and Robert Dean, *A Holy Rebellion.* Eugene, OR: Harvest House, 1990. See Ice and Dean for a thorough, biblical defense of this position.

[3]Neil Anderson, *Victory Over the Darkness.* Ventura, CA: Regal, 1990, p. 10

[4]Ibid., p. 43–44.

[5]Ibid. See pp. 45–47 for a complete statement of who we are in Christ.

[6]Neil Anderson, *The Bondage Breaker.* Eugene, OR: Harvest House, 1990, p. 172.

[7]Ibid, p. 179.

[8]This is what the tense of the verb *sins* indicates.

[9]W. Bauer, W. F. Arndt, F. W. Gingrich, *Greek-English Lexicon.* Chicago, IL: U of Chicago Press, 1957, p. 102.

[10]William Lawrence, *The Traitor in the Gates: The Christian's Conflict with the Flesh.* Essays in Honor of J. Dwight Pentecost, Stanley Toussaint and Charles Dyer, ed., Chicago: Moody Press, 1986, p. 124.

[11]David Needham, *Birthright.* Portland, OR: Multnomah, 1979, p. 139.

[12]F. F. Bruce, *Commentary on Galatians.* Grand Rapids, MI: Eerdman's, 1982, p. 243.

[13]William Lawrence, p. 128.

7. Emotional Trauma and Discipleship

NOT long ago I was interviewed about my book *Why Christians Sin* by a radio station personality in Southern California. During the course of the interview I explained that because the Spirit indwells us, empowers us, and leads us into what is right, we cannot blame the world, the flesh, or the devil when we consciously sin. We make the choice to do what we know is wrong. In addition, I explained that the only reason a true believer would choose a lifestyle of sin is because of serious disappointment with God.

At this point the interviewer was clearly disturbed by what I said. She implied that my explanation of why Christians sin was simplistic. She then suggested that sometimes Christians are so broken by physical or emotional abuse that they cannot do what is right. I qualified what I was saying by admitting that when believers are hurting or suffering, it can be extremely difficult to obey God, and obedience may come very slowly—in small, painful steps. I also pointed out that sometimes a hurting believer does not know exactly what God wants him or her to do. Nevertheless, I had to respectfully disagree with any suggestion that Christians cannot obey because they are emotionally traumatized. Unfortunately, that effectively ended the interview.

Looking back, I wish I'd had the time to explain, logically and biblically, why I so firmly believe that Christians sometimes will not do what is right, but why we should not say believers sometimes cannot obey what God says.

First of all, some Christians suffer emotional anguish that is, humanly speaking, impossible to bear. And what some believers have suffered in this life is more than I can fully comprehend. I see these hurting people on a regular basis for counsel, sympathy, and help. Hardly a day goes by that I don't cry with people about some situation that has broken their hearts, and mine. These people need all the help, support, and sympathy we can give them. But at the same time we must lovingly correct any mention or notion that they cannot do what is right and best for them. If we do not, logically and practically, we have stepped onto a very slippery slope.

I can understand why forgiveness would be difficult for a boy whose growing-up years were marked by daily beatings from his father. My heart admits that perhaps, in a case like this, forgiveness is impossible. And in fact, this case is not hypothetical.

I spent a couple of days at a Prison Fellowship Seminar with a man called "Animal" by the guards and other inmates. He was about six feet five inches and roughly 300 pounds. He was also one of the angriest and most bitter persons I have ever met. He told me that his father beat him up nearly every day until he was twenty-one. When I asked him what happened after that he said with satisfaction, "I finally had enough and I put my old man in the hospital for two months." I can almost accept this man's emotional inability to forgive his father.

But a red flag went up for me when another man said he cannot forgive his wife of twenty years for constantly burning his toast. We must assert that this man's emotional suffering is not in the same category as the abused boy's, but who are we to judge? Once the criteria of emotional duress is introduced, it is very difficult to draw a line anywhere and determine what legitimately prevents a Christian from obeying God's Word. If a person says that years of burnt toast have wiped him out emotionally, how can we argue with him? Only he and God really know the extent of his emotional pain. Fortunately, God's Word provides a definitive explanation of why Christians can obey God, even under tremendous emotional duress.

In 1 Corinthians 10:13, the apostle Paul says:

> No temptation has overtaken you but such as is common to man; and God is faithful, who will not allow you to be tempted beyond what you are able, but with the temptation will provide the way of escape also, that you may be able to endure it.

The word *temptation* in this verse can refer to either Satan's temptation or God's testing.[1] The context determines the proper translation. However, in a sense the issue of translation is moot. When Satan tempts us, God allows it as a divine test, and whenever God tests us, Satan will seize the opportunity to tempt us to sin.[2] The point is that both satanic temptation and divine testing are ultimately in view in 1 Corinthians 10:13. The promise of this verse is that God will not allow us to be tempted or tested beyond what we are able to endure.

The word *able* indicates that we have the power and ability (because of God's indwelling Spirit) to endure any testing and temptation. We *can* resist Satan and do what God wants us to do. Thus, on the basis of God's Word, we have to say that no matter how bad things are, Christians should and can obey God. Besides, it is only through obedience to God that genuine and lasting healing can come to those who hurt so much. In saying this I am not saying that struggling Christians simply need to be counseled to obey God. There are situations when counseling, no matter how correct and well carried out, is just not going to be enough.

The added ingredient

When the woman first came to see me, it was all she could do just to drag herself into my office. Her pain and hopelessness were evident from her face and appearance. She didn't really care if she lived or died. Her husband decided that he didn't love her anymore, and he discarded her like a pair of worn-out socks. To make matters worse, many people she thought would support and help her failed her miserably. She had seen a physician who had prescribed antidepressant drugs for her, but she had been on this medication for some time and still was depressed. It appeared to this Christian woman that God, too, had abandoned her and that no one could or would come to her rescue. She felt at the end of her rope. Her question was, could I help her? My answer was yes, but not through counseling alone.

There are times when counseling, any counseling, is simply not enough. I am not saying that counseling is not necessary, but I am saying that there are many occasions when Christians who are hurting and struggling need something in addition to counseling. That something is *discipleship*.

Now before I explain from Scripture what I am referring to by the term "discipling," let me say that I am aware that there are people who say that discipling has been tried in the past and has failed. Bruce Narramore, dean of Rosemead Graduate School of Psychology, says, "I think the critics need to ask, 'Why are people so interested in psychology?' The thought is that we ought to go back to the old way. But the old way wasn't working. The church wasn't stemming the tide."[3]

I am not advocating a return to the "old way." I realize, as a third-generation pastor, that in the past the church has given insufficient or pat answers to complicated human problems. I also believe that even though many evangelical fundamental churches thought that they were doing biblical discipleship, not many of them actually were—in the past or are today. The problem is not that discipleship has been tried and found wanting; rather discipleship has been wanted but has remained largely untried. The church needs to go back to Scripture to see what biblical discipleship really involves, and then begin to practice it, particularly among Christians who are struggling with spiritual/emotional problems.

The apostle Paul, in 1 Thessalonians 2:7–12, says,

> We proved to be gentle among you, as a nursing mother
> tenderly cares for her own children. Having thus a fond
> affection for you, we were well pleased to impart to you
> not only the gospel but also our own lives, because you
> had become very dear to us. For you recall, brethren,
> our labor and hardship, how working night and day so
> as not to be a burden to any of you, we proclaimed to
> you the gospel of God.

Paul knew that in order for the Thessalonians to be motivated to change and grow they had to be convinced that he cared about them personally. Therefore, he handled them gently like a nursing mother (2:7). He also spent time with them sharing his life with them, in addition to sharing God's truth with them (2:8). To further establish a context of love, Paul and those with him made tents to support themselves financially so they would not be a financial burden to the Thessalonians (2:9). The result of all this was that the Thessalonian believers knew Paul loved them and they responded positively to his discipling ministry and became imitators of Paul and of Christ (1:6).

Sometimes through empathy with the counselee, a counselor can establish a context of love that motivates the client to listen and be willing to change and grow. However, in some situations, empathy cannot be adequately communicated, or the time it takes to communicate it in counseling is unacceptably long. In these situations, discipleship is crucial in reaching out to those who need help.

There is a man I know who was hurting terribly. His pain was partly due to longstanding marital problems and his sinful attempts to deal with them. Several years ago I offered to counsel with him but he kindly refused my offer. I wasn't sure of his reason then, but I know now. He didn't doubt my credentials or competence, he wondered if I truly cared about him. He wanted to be sure that I didn't view him as just another person who needed to be "straightened out." So to establish a context of love I invited him to a small discipleship group and he accepted. In this group we shared our joys and concerns, we prayed for each other, and we studied God's Word together. In the midst of this discipling relationship he became convinced that I cared about him as a person, not just a counselee. As a result, he came to see me for counseling, and he came ready to change and grow. That's what a discipling relationship provides that a counseling relationship sometimes does not: the context of a loving relationship.

In 1 Thessalonians 2:10, the second important element in the discipling process is found. It has to do with modeling the truth. Paul says, "You are witnesses, and so is God, how devoutly and uprightly and blamelessly we behaved toward you believers."

Paul indicates that he and the others in the apostolic band were a model of proper Christian living. They didn't just tell the Thessalonian believers how to live the Christian life, they showed them how to live it. Paul also refers to his example in 2 Thessalonians 3:7 where he says, "You yourselves know how you ought to follow our example." The key word here is *how*. One of the major weaknesses of most counseling is that it does not provide specific, concrete examples of how to deal with life's problems. What the counselee usually gets is general exhortations and verbal examples. It's one thing to tell one what to do, it's another thing to show one how to do it. So much often gets lost in the translation. The application of biblical truth to life is so much easier and more effective when it is modeled and demonstrated, rather than simply explained. This is something else that discipling provides that counseling often doesn't.

The third element in discipling has to do with accountability and support. These two things go hand in hand, and when you have one the other can and should be there as well. In 1 Thessalonians 2:11–12, Paul shows what accountability and support is all about:

> . . . you know how we were exhorting and encouraging and imploring each one of you as a father would his own children, so that you may walk in a manner worthy of the God who calls you into His own kingdom and glory.

Paul says he exhorted, encouraged, and implored them to do what was right and best like a good father would. Implied in these words and this imagery is, first of all, support. He was there for them when they needed him. He was available to encourage and help the Thessalonian Christians do what they needed to do. The word *exhorting* indicates a personal urging as well as an expression of encouraging words.[4]

This passage also implies accountability. Paul was aware of what the Thessalonians were and were not doing, and was not afraid to insist that they do what was right and best. That is what the word *imploring* indicates.[5] He insisted that they do what would bring honor to God, and they were clearly willing to be accountable to him.

When people are struggling with severe spiritual/emotional problems, they either need someone with them all the time to help and support them or they need someone available at critical times. But these hurting people also need to be accountable to that person so that the support person knows how to help them and appropriately can insist that they follow through with their part of the healing process.

When counseling is not enough, one of the common causes is a lack of support and accountability. Often the primary reason is not the unwillingness of the counselee to be supported and accountable, but the fact that counseling is not designed to accommodate either one. Usually the counselor and client meet in an office for regularly scheduled appointments that can be separated by days or even weeks. This is another reason why counseling *and* discipling are necessary. How then can a counselor help those who require both counseling and discipling? Let me go back to the woman whose husband left her alone and depressed.

In that situation I realized that the woman required counseling as well as medication for her depression. She needed counsel about how to cope with being single again after so many years of marriage, and she needed someone to help her understand where God was in the midst of all she was going through. At the time I was able and willing to provide the necessary counsel, but she needed discipling as well. I asked her if she would be willing to meet at least once a week for Bible study and prayer with a mature Christian woman. I told her that she could call this person any time she needed encouragement or prayer, but she would also have to be accountable to her for her thoughts and behavior. The troubled woman knew the person I mentioned and immediately agreed.

I met with the discipler and explained the plan for healing and her role in the process. In addition, I put the hurting woman in touch with a co-dependency support group at our church. So between the medication she received from a qualified physician, my own counseling efforts, the insight she gained from the discipler, the encouragement and prayers offered by others in the church, and, of course, with the help of God's Word and His Spirit, this woman is successfully addressing her problems and growing as a person. Life still hurts, but she is experiencing hope and growth in the midst of her trauma.

Twelve-step programs

How do twelve-step programs and recovery ministries fit into the discipling dimension? Twelve-step programs that point people to Christ (not just to a "higher power") provide necessary accountability and support. Christian recovery clinics and ministries also provide helpful accountability and support. These programs and ministries are better in that aspect than counseling alone when Christians are struggling with certain kinds of sins and problems. But twelve-step programs and recovery ministries sometimes suffer the same weakness as some Christian counseling by stressing empathy at the expense of biblical direction and application, particularly in one crucial area.

In Galatians 6:1, Paul says:

> Brethren, even if a man is caught in any trespass, you
> who are spiritual, restore such a one in a spirit of gentle-

ness, each one looking to yourselves, lest you too be
tempted.

The word *caught* means "to take before(hand)."[6] It combines
the elements of surprise as well as capture. A good translation
of it would be "ensnared." Paul is saying here that sometimes
we as Christians are trapped by sin, and when this happens,
Christians who are "spiritual" enough to recognize it need to
help "restore" that believer.

The word *restore* has the idea of returning someone or
something to its original state, and this word was often used in
the sense of mending or resetting a broken bone.[7] In other
words, it refers to helping fellow Christians escape from sin
with all its negative consequences, and the restoration of fellowship with God with all its positive benefits.

The way *restore* is used here can indicate a process
rather than a one-time event, and I believe that this is usually
the case.[8] The process of restoration always includes
approaching a person ensnared in sin with a "spirit of gentleness." This involves conveying love for the person as well as
acknowledging one's own tendency to sin. But this process of
restoration may also include helping the person with problems
related to the sin. The verse immediately following Galatians
6:1 says, "Bear one another's burdens, and thus fulfill the law
of Christ" (6:2). Part of the process of restoration may include
counseling people about situations and problems that didn't
cause them to sin but may have contributed to their willingness to sin and that set the stage for it. Nevertheless, sin must
be dealt with in order for people to be restored to wholeness.

Some Christian twelve-step groups or recovery ministries are reticent to confront hurting people about their sin.
But even when they are willing to confront sinful thoughts
and behavior, that may not be enough. The Christian ensnared
in sin may not be willing to deal with his or her sin and begin

doing what is right and best, even when approached by a group in a spirit of gentleness.

In their book *Worry-Free Living,* Drs. Hawkins, Meier, and Minirth say,

> We once asked our staff of counselors to estimate how many of their patients come to our clinic to learn the truth about themselves so that they can do something to correct whatever is wrong. The therapists' best guesstimate was that only 25% of all Minirth-Meier clients want to find out the truth, and even fewer want to deal with it. Most patients visit the clinic looking for quick and easy solutions. They want a pill to make their anxiety go away. Or they want a counselor to listen to their problems and to blame the problems on someone else. The last thing a patient wants to hear is that his own anger or guilt or jealousy is the source of his anxiety and that he is responsible for getting rid of the negative emotion.[9]

These counselors contend that no more than one-fourth of those looking for help want to know the truth about their problems. Although this is very difficult to prove, I believe that it is accurate. Few Christians are willing to admit that they don't want to know what God's Word says. Still fewer are willing to admit that they believe God's Word is wrong, or simply won't work in their case. A lot of hurting Christians choose to think that their situation is different or the exception. Yet, in many cases, they know that Scripture is true and that God was aware of all exceptions when He gave us His Word.

Most Christians believe that if they admit to a counselor that they are disappointed with God and His Word, their counseling will effectively end and the blame for their problems and their failure to get better will rest squarely on their own shoulders. Therefore, while they pay lip service to the truth of

Scripture and the need to accept it, many Christians quietly refuse to accept or act on biblical counsel. Why?

One counselor says the reason is that these Christians have rationalized their disregard of God's Word.[10] This is undoubtedly true, but why are people looking for ways to justify themselves and their condition? The first answer is lack of faith.

The Bible indicates in 1 Thessalonians 5:14 that there are some Christians who are *fainthearted*. This term refers to people who are genuine believers who have genuine faith in God, but their faith is small and limited. Because of the way they lived before they trusted Christ and because of their spiritual immaturity, these people have a difficult time believing God can help them, particularly in certain areas of their lives. Even several counseling sessions using Scripture with these Christians may not prove successful. These people require much patience and encouragement from fellow believers to grow in their faith (1 Thess. 5:14). Nevertheless, I believe that only a small number of Christians are truly "fainthearted." A far greater number of believers are simply unwilling to accept God's Word because they are disappointed with God. How then can we overcome genuine disappointment with God and recover faith in Him and hope for our situation? That critical issue will be addressed in chapter 8.

Questions for Reflection and Action

1. Do you believe that you have been emotionally traumatized by something or someone? If so, are you able to state what happened and why the incident(s) were so devastating to you emotionally?

2. Are you doing what is biblically right and tapping into God's resources or are you dealing with your pain in a sinful way?

3. Are you in a personal or small group discipling situation where there is love, modeling of biblical truth, accountability and support, or are you simply being counseled?

4. Can you honestly say that you want to get better emotionally and that you are willing to do whatever God indicates it will take? If not, have you asked yourself why not?

Notes

[1] W. Bauer, W. F. Arndt, F. W. Gingrich, *Greek-English Lexicon*, Chicago, IL: U of Chicago Press, 1957, p. 646.

[2] For a real-life illustration of this truth, reread the book of Job.

[3] Bruce Narramore, "The Therapeutic Revolution," *Christianity Today*, May 17, 1993, p. 29.

[4] W. Bauer, W. F. Arndt, F. W. Gingrich, p. 622.

[5] D. Edmond Hiebert, *The Thessalonian Epistles.* Chicago: Moody Press, 1971, p. 104.

[6] W. Bauer, W. F. Arndt, F. W. Gingrich, p. 715.

[7] J. B. Lightfoot,*The Epistle of St. Paul to the Galatians.* Nashville, TN: Thomas Nelson, 1989, p. 289.

[8] Donald Guthrie, *Galatians.* Grand Rapids, MI: Eerdman's, 1981, p. 142.

[9] Donald Hawkins, Paul Meier, and Frank Minirth, *Worry-Free Living.* Nashville, TN: Thomas Nelson, 1989, p. 28–29.

[10] Jay Adams, *Christian Counselor's Manual.* Phillipsburg, NJ: Presbyterian & Reformed, 1973, p. 23.

8. From Disappointment to Discovery

IF you or someone you love has "tried everything" and yet continues to be overwhelmed by problems, listen to the words of Christian psychologist William Backus in his book *The Hidden Rift With God:*

> In my counseling practice, I've heard these words—"I've tried everything"—many times from those who have never quite recovered from the sudden loss of a loved one, or from the disclosure of a spouse's illicit affair, or a rudely shut door of opportunity, or turning forty. Many of these folks have tried to anesthetize themselves with alcohol, while others "soften the blow" with drugs. Others get "into" pseudo-spiritual movements, reciting whistle-in-the-dark, every-cloud-has-a-silver-lining, it'll-all-come-out-in-the-wash-so-cheer-up phrases, only to discover that they're hollow. Some try pouring on Christian practices: "I'll go to church more, pray longer, give more." Most have not

overlooked counseling. They go to their pastors asking
for help, and many pastors give themselves generously
(sometimes more generously than they can afford) to
the cure of individual souls. This ministry succeeds in
building faith and resolving the difficulties of many.
But too often, pastors are left with frustration when the
one they are counseling will not or cannot be helped.
Psychologists and psychiatrists, too, encounter individuals they are unable to help, and many of them cannot
conceive that the true field of conflict lies deeper than
the unconscious mind. So, even after wearing out several pastors and counselors, the desperate, hurting soul
sometimes says, "I've tried everything. NOTHING
helps." When nothing works—and nothing else is a
true, permanent solution—I maintain that it's time to go
deeper.[1]

Dr. Backus has helped a great many people and has written several popular books designed to enable struggling
Christians to help themselves, and he says, "When nothing
works . . . it's time to go deeper." I agree. But the question is,
deeper into what?

When Christians seem to make no progress with their
problems and have tried everything, the root issue is almost
certainly their relationship with God. More specifically, they
are angry with Him. In some cases, the believer genuinely
may not realize the extent of his or her anger toward God. But
in most situations, one knows deep down that one is upset
with God but does not want to admit it to oneself or to others.
Again Backus observes:

Most people think that anger at God is too hot to
handle. At some level they may know they have a
quarrel, a separation, a falling out with God, but they
cover it because it's too terrible to admit. Why is it too

terrible? Because of fear. What would God do if He knew . . . ? What would that say about me as a person? As a Christian? What our anger at God really reveals is that at the base of our beliefs (what we consciously say we believe) lies another level of thought (what we really believe). And when what we really believe separates us from God, then we are suffering from misbeliefs.[2]

What are these "misbeliefs"? Whenever a Christian is angry or disappointed with God, that person typically has serious doubts about either the power of God or the goodness of God. The angry Christian may not completely lose faith in God in either one of these two areas, but he or she often harbors important doubts. In other words, the angry Christian's faith in God's power or goodness may be real, but it is not what it needs to be for healing to occur.

When a Christian with sufficient faith in God's power and goodness encounters difficult or painful situations, that person will definitely hurt and almost certainly struggle for a while with questions and doubts about God. However, faith in God's control and love will keep him or her from developing deep-seated anger toward God. Trust and joy will support this individual.

But when a Christian does not have sufficient faith in both God's power and goodness during life's most perplexing and painful experiences, that believer will begin to doubt seriously either God's power or love, and those doubts can eventually lead to deep anger and disappointment with God. Larry Crabb tells a story in *Finding God* that illustrates this point:

> One Wednesday evening after choir practice,
> Carol, a middle-aged single woman, walked alone to
> her car in the church parking lot. A sixteen-year-old
> boy emerged from the shadows, forced her into her car
> at gunpoint, made her drive to a deserted spot in the

woods, and for the next twenty-four hours coerced her to engage in vile and perverted sexual activity. He then left the car and ran off. In a professional office two days later, a therapist asked her to relive the horrors of that day by visualizing, with closed eyes, all that happened, but to imagine Jesus there with her. The technique was meant to heal Carol's painful memory. Instead, she immediately lost control and screamed, "That's just the problem. I already believe he was there. Why didn't he do anything?"[3]

Many hurting believers say, "I was angry with God, but now I'm just very disappointed with Him." This is where a lot of angry Christians eventually end up. They may start out being angry with God because they conclude that He isn't as loving or as powerful as He should be. But they often move from anger to disappointment. They are deeply hurt that God has failed them, but they realize that one cannot fight with God, so they simply resign themselves to their painful circumstances. This does not improve their lives or their relationship with God.

Quite the contrary, disillusioned Christians experience a very strained relationship with God. They often fall into willful sin for significant periods of time. Disappointed Christians never completely lose their faith, nor do they quit professing Christ. They still believe, but their faith is small and they stumble about as "walking wounded."

Sometimes counseling and discipleship can help a Christian who is angry or disillusioned with God. If a counselor correctly understands and points out what the root problem is, and a discipler demonstrates Jesus' love and encourages the struggling Christian to trust God and His Word, it is possible to lead these believers back into a close relationship with God. But this doesn't happen very often. When a Christian gets to the point where one is angry or disillusioned with God, one must usually have a fresh encounter with the living God. He or she will need to rediscover God, particularly His power and goodness.

Peter's Pattern

In John 21:1–19, we have an example of a disillusioned Christian who rediscovered Christ—and the result is life-changing.

At least twice during Jesus' earthly ministry Peter acted as spokesman for the disciples and affirmed his faith in Jesus as the son of God (Matt. 16:16; John 6:68–69). There should be no doubt that Peter was a genuine Christian even though he did wrongly deny Jesus (Matt. 26:69–74). Nevertheless, he was clearly angry about Jesus' having to go to the cross (Matt. 16:22; John 18:10–11), and he apparently became disillusioned with God even though Jesus was resurrected from the dead. We do not know why. We can only speculate. Perhaps Peter was disappointed by the fact that Jesus did not immediately establish His promised kingdom on earth after the resurrection. Whatever the actual reason, Peter's return to fishing indicates that he was indeed disillusioned with God.

As we see from the account, the disciples fished all night and caught nothing. Just as day was breaking, Jesus appeared on the beach and called out to them. They did not know it was He who asked them if they had netted any fish. When they said no, Jesus told them to lower their nets on the right hand side of the boat. The result was miraculous, both in terms of the number of fish in their net as well as Peter's reaction.

When John told Peter that Jesus was on the beach, he tied up his outer garment and swam for shore, even though it was a hundred yards away (John 21:8). Jesus' incredible demonstration of power and goodness touched Peter dramatically that day, just as it did almost three years before when he first realized exactly who Jesus was (Luke 5:1–11). At that time Peter doubted Jesus' power and goodness, and on that occasion Jesus miraculously filled his net with fish. Peter responded by falling at Jesus' feet and crying out, "Depart from me, for I am a sinful man, O Lord!" (Luke 5:8).

John 21 shows that Christians can become disillusioned with God and that often it takes a fresh encounter with Him to get these believers on the path to restoration. When Christians have serious doubts about God's power or goodness, they need to rediscover God as He really is in order to truly begin dealing with their problems. But the question is, how does one rediscover God?

Recovery requires rediscovery

The place to start is in God's Word and in prayer. The Bible is God's written revelation of Himself to us, and God often speaks to us as we commune with Him in prayer. But it is not enough to simply read the Scripture and pray as a duty, discipline, or academic exercise. In order to meet with God in a fresh way, the believer must approach God's Word and prayer with priority and passion. Listen to how one author beautifully describes the way we must pursue God:

> We find God to the degree that we want to find
> him. Until our passion for finding God exceeds all other
> passions, and until we long to know him as our Lord and
> friend more than to use him to get what we want (the
> way a spoiled child uses a rich father), we will not find
> him as deeply as he longs to be found. He will not reveal
> himself to us in those wonderful glimpses of his love or
> in that quiet reassurance that he is with us.[4]

God wants to let us find Him. Especially when years of living as Christians have seemingly brought us no closer to

Him, God delights to be discovered. He is not playing hard to get. Something about the way we are and who He is makes it necessary for us to want Him more than we want anyone or anything else before we can find Him. " 'You will seek Me and find Me when you search for Me with all your heart. And I will found by you,' declares the Lord" (Jer. 29:13–14a).

We must put a priority on rediscovering God and it must be a passion for us. The place we begin looking for Him is in God's Word and in prayer. But God is not limited to these avenues, nor can we force Him to disclose Himself to us within our time frame. God allows us glimpses of His incredible power and marvelous love when and where He chooses. Again, Larry Crabb puts it well when he says:

> God remains absolutely independent, disclosing himself when he chooses. But now his unpredictability becomes delightful, simply because you have seen him. You know what he is like. You trust him to do whatever is good because you know he is good. As long as this confidence remains, you experience a peace beneath your worst trial, an eagerness to love in spite of mistreatment, and a joy deeper than your deepest sorrow
>
> You still struggle, sometimes severely, with fear, anger, and discouragement. But now a quiet awareness will not fully go away, an awareness that God is good, that sin is bad, and that the relief it brings is temporary and, in the long run, futile. You find yourself a little more patient. You check irritability when it rises. You are confident, even in the middle of panic, that things will be all right. You actually begin to believe the Lord when he says, "But take courage; I have overcome the world" (John 16:33). You rest in the guarantee that all the badness of the world will never overcome God's goodness.[5]

The bottom line is that disappointed Christians need to rediscover God in order to begin to have victory over life's struggles. This often occurs when reading God's Word or praying if we do so with a passion for knowing God. But God is not limited to these times or ways.

Someone might rightly ask—what about the Holy Spirit? How can a Christian become disillusioned if she or he is indwelt with God's Spirit, and what is the Spirit's role in a believer's rediscovery of God?

It is true that all believers are indwelt by the Holy Spirit (Rom. 8:9). It is also true that the Spirit can be "quenched" (1 Thess. 5:19). When a Christian becomes disappointed with God, that is, when one begins to have serious doubts about God's power or love, one often begins to resist the Spirit's ministry in one's life. How we can do this is amazing (Acts 5:4), and yet the Bible affirms that it is indeed possible. Nevertheless, the Spirit's work in our lives is never completely extinguished. The Holy Spirit continues to work in us, both to urge and to enable us to do what is right (Phil. 2:13). God's Spirit strongly urges the disillusioned believer to rediscover God, and it is the Holy Spirit who ultimately guides us into rediscovering the truth of who God really is (John 16:13).

Read carefully the words of a man who was angry with God and who had "tried everything" to deal with his problems:

> He had betrayed me, let me down, failed to protect me, ignored my record of faithful service and broken all promises to hear and answer prayer. He had chosen what was bad for me, and not something good. Underneath it all, I had a big, hot disagreement with God. A major rift. I can remember the anger breaking out into rage one night when I was driving home from a party I have long since forgotten. I don't even recall what trivial frustration had set off the outburst of fury, but I re-

member well how violently I stormed and shouted at God. But God is in the business of healing spiritual rifts—rebuilding broken bridges if we will only let Him. For me, the first approach happened this way.

I heard a rumor that a friend had a life-revolution-izing experience with God. That was ridiculous! An experience with God? Something to do with the Holy Spirit? Definitely weird. God never did anything palpable in our time, and I decided my friend's experience was some form of self-deception or hysteria.

Yet I remembered something that gave me pause—hadn't another friend written to me of a similar experience? He said God had become "real" to him and turned his life and pastoral ministry around. It couldn't hurt to find out a little more. I began to read books and listen to tapes that made this claim: Anyone who truly calls upon God, no matter what his personal state, can experience His love, His forgiveness and His presence. A dozen conflicting thoughts and emotions rose in me. I was a confirmed Christian: I believed in the Father, Son and Holy Spirit, no question. What were these people talking about? Why should I believe these reports when God had so let me down?

On the other hand, my life was a mess. What did I have to lose? Skeptically, and with many reservations, I began prayer something like, "Please give me that experience too. But when and if you do, God don't make things too difficult."

Nothing happened. Of course not. I smirked. Then a third friend came for a visit. He also claimed he'd experienced "the reality of the living God." He even insisted that God does miracles today! "It's all coincidence, illusion, and the power of suggestion!" I argued. He reminded me of God's great love for me in sending His Son to die a terrible death on a cross. Though I knew that intellectually, it did no good.

On the last morning of his visit, in the middle of an argument, something happened that was totally different from anything I'd experienced in my forty-five years of life. I was arguing (for my own position and against "all this scriptural stuff") when I suddenly fell silent in mid-sentence. Quite literally, the speech centers of my brain were actually vacant. No words were there. I moved my lips, but instead the tears began to flow, and in a moment I was sobbing.

Here was the really odd thing: I felt a new kind of sorrow—not pity for myself, but a grieving over what I had done with God! Because I was suffering, I had turned on Him, doubted Him, blamed Him and hardened myself against Him. I was angry. There was a rift between us and I now saw that I had created it. I had been so wrong about Him.

That morning I asked God to forgive me, to cleanse me and to restore—not my lost family and possessions but my soul. But it was when my friends prayed for me that it occurred.

At first there was only a waiting silence. Then, He was unmistakably there, just as His Word promises He will be, and I felt His holy presence. For the first time, I really felt His love—directly, perceptibly, in the center of my being. I sensed His nearness and His willingness to heal the rift between us, notwithstanding all I had done to widen it. He came to me in spite of my unbelief, my furious rebellion, even my deliberate decisions to do wrong.

For many days and weeks after, when I opened the Bible to read the words vibrated with life. More than that, I knew in the core of my being that these words were true no matter what the "scientific" critics said. My heart was changed, and now I wanted to please Him even more than I wanted those things I'd considered previous above all else—and to trust Him no matter what.[6]

This man who rediscovered God is William Backus, the psychologist quoted at the beginning of this chapter. He tried everything, but nothing worked until he had a fresh encounter with the living God.

When you have tried everything to deal with your problems and nothing seems to work, you may very well be angry or disillusioned with God. If so, the answer may come through counseling or discipleship, but often it comes through rediscovering the power and goodness of God. When you see God afresh, as He really is, your trust in Him will return to a level where you can begin to make progress in life again. You can then begin to experience victory in the midst of your struggles, even though your struggles do not completely disappear.

Questions for Reflection and Action

1. Is it possible you are angry with God? If so, try to articulate why. If not, could it be that you feel disillusioned with or hurt by God? If so, why is this the case?
2. Do you have some doubts about either the power or goodness of God? If so, what are they?
3. If God seems distant and confusing to you, have you asked Him to show Himself to you through His Word and prayer?
4. Do you want to rediscover God? Is this something that you desire with all your heart?

Notes

[1] William Backus, *The Hidden Rift with God*. Minneapolis, MN: Bethany House, 1990, p. 35–36.
[2] Ibid., p. 39.
[3] Larry Crabb, *Finding God*. Grand Rapids, MI: Zondervan, 1993, p. 186.
[4] See the author's book, *Why Christians Sin,* particularly chapter 4, for a full discussion of this issue.
[5] Larry Crabb, p. 186.
[6] William Backus, p. 26–28.

9. Victory In The Midst Of Struggle

JONI Eareckson Tada is a spiritual role model to Christians all over the world. Even though she was paralyzed in a diving accident at the age of seventeen, she has not allowed that terrible incident to defeat her. By relying on God and utilizing all of her talents and abilities, she has lived a life of victory. But her victorious life has not been without tremendous struggle, and she readily admits in her book, *Choices and Changes,* that she has had her share of defeats. Joni also recognizes that short-term defeats are always possible even in the midst of long-term victory:

> I reread my book, *A Step Further,* with great interest, swallowing the advice Steve and I wrote for others to read. I notice in the introduction the words, "Oh, I'm still paralyzed . . . But I'm no longer depressed." I smile at the confidence with which I penned that phrase. Little did I realize then that depression would one day hit me so hard. And I cannot presume that it will never return. I called my editor and asked her to delete that line in the next printing.[1]

When Christians struggle to gain victory over their problems, the root issue is often disillusionment with God. The solution, therefore, is for these hurting people to rediscover God's power and love. But even if one rediscovers God and then begins to experience victory over the problems that have plagued one, this does not mean that life from then on will be free of struggle and pain.

The thrill of victory

Many Christians continue to labor under two erroneous assumptions. The first is that Christians who trust God fully can arrive at a point where they no longer struggle. The belief in the "victorious Christian life" without problems or pain is, unfortunately, one to which many Christians still cling.

In his book, *Living With Everyday Problems,* Eugene Kennedy says this:

> If I can just get through this problem, then everything will be all right," may be one of the most common English sentences. But there comes a time, and it may well be the birth of maturity—when we suddenly realize that if we do get through our present problem, there will be another one, slightly larger and a little more intense, waiting to take its place.[2]

He is right because what he says confirms what Jesus said in John 16:33, "In the world you have tribulation . . ." (NKJV). Why is this true? One reason is that we will always have three powerful enemies attacking us each day that we live on this planet: the world, the flesh, and the devil. These three foes engage in a relentless assault on believers. But in addition to these enemies, we live in a fallen world where the consequences of sin are felt by each of us every day. Sin has brought sickness, death, pain, and broken relationships into each of our lives. The result is that all of us are going to struggle because we live in the midst of spiritual warfare and a fallen world.

I realize that there are Christians who do not appear to struggle with anything serious. These people seem to live continuously successful lives. They may even claim that this is the case. I've heard "testimonies," and you probably have as well, from people who state unequivocally that since a certain time or encounter with God everything has been "wonderful" and God has granted them "victory" over all their problems.

I have known enough of these "victorious" Christians personally to make me very skeptical of such claims. It is true that victory in this fallen world is possible through faith in God (1 John 5:4). It is also true that believers can defeat Satan on a regular basis through obedience to God's Word (1 John 2:14). However, continuous and complete victory in this life is never promised us in God's Word, and victory rarely comes without pain and struggle.

Those we observe living without apparent pain or struggle are either living in denial or resignation—the lack of pain or struggle is only apparent, not real.

If a one attempts to deny the pain and struggle of this fallen world, it does not make life any more bearable. It simply cuts that person off from the support and encouragement that one could be receiving if one would admit to God and others that one is hurting and struggling. There are people who claim to be doing "fine" and who refuse to acknowledge the effects of a fallen world on their lives. But don't be fooled, the pain and struggle for these folks is even greater than it is for those who humbly admit their plight and seek help from God and fellow believers who care.

The agony of defeat

In addition to those who refuse to acknowledge their struggles, there are believers who have resigned themselves to defeat. These people sometimes do not seem to struggle because they have temporarily surrendered to the world, flesh, and the devil. These are Christians who instead of engaging in spiritual warfare, have laid down their weapons and have decided not to fight for a while. This spiritual surrender can give some people the outward appearance of being peaceful, in control, and victorious, because they are no longer wrestling with the powers of darkness. But in reality there is an internal conflict raging.

The Spirit of God can be quenched by the believer (1 Thess. 5:19), which means Christians can resist His leading. Nevertheless, the Spirit will continue to urge us to do what is right (Rom. 8:14). Thus a Christian who ceases to do battle with the world, the flesh, and the devil will then begin to struggle with the promptings of the indwelling Spirit. What's more, even though the believer who gives in to sin may initially find some relief and pleasure, this is only temporary (Heb. 11:25). Eventually one is going to realize that one is not getting what one wants out of sin. Surrender to sin is never the answer, though it may appear to be for a time.

The belief that Christians can arrive at a point where victory is continuous and struggles are minimal is sadly mistaken. Those who continue to cling to such thinking are headed for serious disillusionment with both God and the Christian life. But there is a second, equally erroneous belief about victory here and now. This belief is espoused by a growing chorus of voices today which claim that victory in this life is largely unattainable. As one person has stated:

> No matter how well I come to know the Lord, until I actually see Him [in heaven], my life will still be a mess—and so will yours.[3]

It is true that Christians are involved in a "struggle" (Eph. 6:12), but this does not rule out a life that is regularly victorious. As stated earlier, the word *struggle* refers to hand-to-hand combat or a wrestling match. And as a participant in a number of sports, I believe that wrestling is perhaps the most demanding. I know some will disagree with me but I say this because wrestlers have to expend a maximum amount of energy in a very short period of time. What's more, wrestling often inflicts a great deal of pain. It truly is a "struggle." However, a wrestler who is in good physical condition, mentally focused, and able to execute the proper moves can regularly beat his opponents. He may not win all of his matches, and he will not win many without pain, but overall he can be a winner.

The same is true in the Christian life. We will not be continually victorious, nor will our struggle be without hurt and pain. Nevertheless, with God's help we can regularly beat our problems and defeat our spiritual enemies. This is not just true for a few "super" Christians. Victory is available to all who know Jesus as Savior and know Him well. There is also a sense in which Christians are always victorious.

In 2 Corinthians 2:14 Paul says, "Thanks be to God, who always leads us in His triumph in Christ . . . ." What this verse indicates is that "in Christ" we are always winners, because we are ultimately on the winning side. Even if we fail at times, we are a part of God's army and His triumphal procession. Eventually we are going to win the war because of Jesus even if we lose the battle today. This truth should be comforting and encouraging for believers. As Jesus said in John 16:33, "In the world you have tribulation, but take courage; I have overcome the world." We are winners in Jesus and with His help we can be victorious now, but the key to victory is knowing Christ intimately.

Over three hundred years ago Abbas the Great, the Shah of Persia, would frequently disguise himself in order to mingle with ordinary people. Whenever he visited the public baths he would spend time with the old man who stoked the fires. They became friends. The disguised Shah would sit and chat with the old man. They would share their food, thoughts, and feelings.

One day the Shah revealed his true identity. He said, "I am that Shah. I have been with you often and have come to know and appreciate you. You are a good man. Ask whatever you desire and I will give it to you." The old fire-keeper said, "You have eaten my food, rejoiced when I rejoiced, wept when I wept, and shared my burdens. I want nothing but your continued friendship, concern, and understanding. All I want is someone who understands me as I am."[4]

Knowing God

Knowing God intimately is not only the key to victory over personal problems, it is the answer to our deepest needs. Most Christians correctly understand that only God can meet our most important and basic needs. What many believers still do not fully comprehend, however, is that God Himself is what we need. What He offers us is not something outside Himself, He invites us to know Him, the true and living God! And when we begin to know Him well, we not only start to experience victory over our personal problems and enemies, we find that He is the answer to all of our desires and needs as well.

When we spend time with God, meditating on Scripture that tells us what He is like, talking with Him frequently in prayer, and reflecting on how He has worked in our lives again and again, something wonderful begins to happen! First, His power and love assures that we can trust Him with our problems and our lives. But beyond this, we begin to feel significant. We start to feel like somebody. Not because of who we are or what we have done in the world's eyes, but because we know God! Not only this, but we also begin to feel an emotional security that we have never felt before. As we experience God's incredible love for us firsthand, we realize that He will never leave us or forsake us (Heb. 13:5). This is what eternal life is all about, and many Christians have not begun to experience it because they think that eternal life is something that comes from God, when it really comes from *knowing* God.

John 17:3 says, "This is eternal life, that they may know Thee, the only true God, and Jesus Christ whom Thou hast sent." All true Christians "know Christ" in the sense that they know He is God, they know that He is the only way to heaven, and they are trusting in Him alone to save them. However, many believers seem to be foggy about what salvation actually is. Salvation is not just deliverance from eternal condemnation. It is not just a home in heaven. Salvation is the opportunity to spend eternity with Jesus Christ. He is the prize! Eternal life is not primarily something that we get to have or a place that we get to go. Eternal life is the opportunity to be with Jesus Christ forever and to get to know Him as well as a person possibly can know Him! Whatever we receive in terms of temporal satisfaction or heavenly possessions will pale in comparison with the privilege of knowing Jesus on earth and throughout eternity.

It is true that we cannot be physically with Him in this life. But we can begin the process of getting to know Him even now. And to the extent that we know Him in this life, we truly experience eternal life! More specifically, this means we experience victory in the midst of struggle, and we begin to feel truly significant and secure. The fact, however, remains that no human being knows Jesus well enough to continually experience victory and to be completely whole. We will have to wait until we see Him face-to-face for that. Nevertheless, the rewards of knowing Jesus even in an imperfect way here and now are great. That is why Paul says in Philippians 3:10 that his goal was that he "may know Him."

Now it is true that the disillusioned believer will not be willing to pursue God initially; that is why it is God who must pursue the disillusioned Christian—those believers who are overwhelmed by personal problems and doubts about the power and goodness of God. He seeks out these hurting ones in His time and His way and He enables them to rediscover who He truly is. But when one rediscovers God, one is expected, along with the rest of us, to pursue God with passion.

Knowing God well in this life is not an easy or brief task. It requires continued discipline and strong desire. We will not get to know God well if we simply view Him as the One who has the solutions to our problems. We will only know Him intimately when we realize He is the answer to our problems. Then our desire will be strong enough to do what is necessary to know Him, and as a by-product, we will be victorious and whole. But for most of us, our desire to know God is pitifully weak.

There is an ancient story from the days of the desert fathers that describes a young man going out to the hut of an aged monk renowned for his depth of understanding into the ways of God. The young man, in a casual and somewhat flippant tone, said he wanted to know God. Would the old man show him?

The ancient saint said nothing but took the young seeker by the hand to a nearby stream. Leading him into the water, the old man grasped the young man firmly and pushed him under the water. Several seconds passed. With a fierce grip, the aged monk held the casual seeker under. The young man began to push, then to struggle. The old man continued to hold the other below the surface. The young man thrashed violently, then with a mighty heave, thrust himself above the water and inhaled great gasps of air. When his panting had subsided after a few minutes, he turned in bewilderment to the old monk.

The ancient sage, wise in the ways of the Lord and human beings, finally spoke, saying, "When you want God as deeply as you wanted air, only then will you find Him."

Jeremiah 29:13–14 gives us a general biblical principle in regard to knowing God; "You will seek Me and find Me, when you search for Me with all your heart. And I will be found by you."

But what if one does not have a strong desire to know God? Is the situation hopeless? Is there anything that can or should be done to help this person?

There may be some pastors or counselors who believe that if a Christian is not really interested in knowing God well, there is no use attempting to counsel or disciple such a person. But I believe that even though counseling and discipleship are not the complete answer, we must start where people are and encourage them to move toward where they need to be (see Jesus' example in John 4).

If Christians enter into counseling and discipleship and see for themselves that the ultimate answer does not lie in either one of these areas, they may realize that knowing God is what they really need, especially if counselors and disciplers keep pointing them in that direction.

The danger today

We are very impatient with ourselves and with others today. We want maturity *now,* and we keep thinking that we can have it quickly if we just stumble onto the right formula or take the proper course of action. But as Neil Anderson correctly states, "There is no instant maturity; it's a process.[5] Merton Strommen echoes this in his book, *The Five Cries of Youth,* when he says, "The American believes instantaneous solutions are as widespread as the air we breathe. It is often assumed that complex mental, moral, or spiritual processes can be completed instantaneously."[6]

We cannot quickly or easily get to know God or achieve a high level of Christian maturity. Nevertheless, we can get to where we need and want to be if we recognize that it is a long process, but one that is certainly worth it!

Summary

Counseling is not always enough, and neither is discipleship; but if each is used as a means to an end, both can be useful in the process of bringing Christians to maturity. If the goal of counseling and discipleship is not seen just to solve problems, but rather to encourage hurting people to know God better, then counseling and discipleship can be extremely useful in the process of moving people toward God and Christian maturity.

Even though I have just explained that counseling can be useful and important in moving Christians toward knowing God better, I realize that some believers still think that counseling is either unnecessary, unbiblical, or even dangerous—especially if you or someone you love has been counseled but not really helped. Let me take some time in chapter 10 to explain why counseling is necessary and biblical, and why almost every Christian needs counsel at one time or another.

For further reading

I would suggest for further reading two books: *Knowing God* by J. I. Packer and *Finding God* by Larry Crabb. The former deals with who God is and what characterizes people who get to know Him well. The latter addresses the obstacles to finding God while emphasizing the importance of doing so. Together these books provide much help in beginning the process of getting to know God.

Notes

[1]Joni Eareckson Tada, *Choices and Changes*. Grand Rapids, MI: Zondervan, 1986, p. 89.

[2]Eugene Kennedy, *Living With Everyday Problems.*
[3]Larry Crabb, *Finding God.* Grand Rapids, MI: Zondervan, 1993, p. 72.
[4]Lewis Drummond and Baxter, *How To Respond to a Skeptic.* Chicago: Moody, 1986, p. 74–75.
[5]Neil Anderson, *Victory Over the Darkness.* Ventura, CA: Regal, 1990, p. 13.
[6]Merton P. Strommen, *Five Cries of Youth.* San Francisco: Harper, 1988, p. 116.

10. The Need For Counseling

S OME time ago I received an urgent phone call from a man in our church who said that he needed to see me right away. I agreed to meet with him, and we set a time, but I was very apprehensive about the encounter. I figured that I was in trouble and that he was coming to my office to set me straight on a certain matter. He and I had engaged in some emotional discussions about the issue of counseling over the years. I asserted that counseling was an important and thoroughly biblical ministry which the church needed to pursue more vigorously. My belief was, and is, that although evangelism and discipleship are more important and foundational, effective biblical counseling must be a priority in any church that desires to minister to people and encourage them to maturity in Christ.

Squarely on the other side of the issue, this godly man maintained that if the church properly emphasized evangelism and sound doctrine, most of the problems that people have would be take care of themselves, and those who needed additional help would have to seek it outside the church. He believed that Christians have the Holy Spirit and God's Word and these two resources are more than enough for believers to help themselves. He felt that a counseling ministry was unnecessary and that it almost certainly lacked a biblical basis. Knowing all of this, I didn't look forward to his visit. But when he came to see me, I was completely surprised.

When the man walked into my office I could tell he was very disturbed. Pain was clearly etched on his face. He was hurting, and he had not come to me looking for a fight. He was looking for help instead. More specifically, he was looking for insight. He was struggling to understand what God was doing in his life and he was wrestling with the question of sin. He wanted to know what He had done to bring God's wrath upon his family and himself. He was at the end of his rope and wanted more than just answers; he needed comfort and encouragement in order to continue on.

We talked for some time about the character and purposes of God. We discussed the fact of our sinfulness and the reality of God's grace and forgiveness. I reminded him of God's wonderful, personal love, and I expressed my own love and concern for him.

Then I addressed his concern about an unknown sin that he thought must be present in his life. I asked him if he had sincerely and specifically prayed for God to show him any sin that he might be unaware of or denying. He told me that prayed David's prayer in Psalm 139:23–24:

> Search me, O God, and know my heart;
> Try me and know my anxious thoughts;

And see if there be any hurtful way in me,
And lead me in the everlasting way.

Believing him to be truthful and sincere, I assured him that if he really wanted God to show him an unknown or suppressed sin, God would do so. And since God had not, I had to conclude that whatever God was doing in his life, it was not to discipline him for sin or to expose sin in his life.

When our time together grew to a close, I felt that each of us had been encouraged and had grown as Christians. There was also a real bond established between us. A trust had been built that would lay the foundation for future discussions. I am not sure if he considered what took place "counseling," but what happened was definitely blessed by God, and it was thoroughly based on Scripture.

Why counseling?

In spite of the widespread embracing of counseling as a legitimate ministry by much of the church, some Christians still view it as suspect. The conviction of many of these believers is that if a Christian needs spiritual/emotional aid, all the individual needs to do is to obey Scripture and rely on God's Spirit. A related conviction has to do with the perception that "counseling" does not have explicit biblical sanction. For instance, nowhere in the Bible does God call the church to "counsel" or command Christians to "counsel."

In response, I would have to admit that, theoretically, one could get along just fine without any outside human help if one knew God's Word perfectly and if one never quenched God's Spirit. But I have not yet met such a Christian. The fact is that we all sometimes quench the Spirit, both knowingly and unknowingly.

In 1 Thessalonians 5:19, Paul tells the Thessalonian Christians, "Do not quench the Spirit." Careful study of the word *quench* shows that this was something they had already been doing for some time, and thus this verse could be translated, "Stop quenching the Spirit."[1] However, if one reads Paul's entire first letter to the Thessalonians, it becomes clear that overall he is pleased with their Christian growth and behavior, even though they were young believers. It appears from the immediate context that the problem was that they were rejecting all "prophetic utterances" (5:20).

While it is clear that the Thessalonians were quenching the Spirit, what is not clear is whether or not they realized it. Were they engaged in deliberate sin and suppression of the truth, or were they simply unaware as new Christians that the prophetic utterances in their midst were the work of the Spirit? Either interpretation is possible.

One can be committing a sin and not realize it if one thinks that one's guilt is due to an overly-strict conscience (1 John 3:21) or if one is ignorant of what God's Word says in that particular area. In this type of situation, God often uses a human counselor to confront the sinning individual and expose the sin using God's Word. And this could very well be what Paul is doing in 1 Thessalonians 5:19–20.[2]

On the other hand, if one is deliberately quenching the Spirit and knowingly committing a sin, then God may also use a human counselor to confront the individual and to expose one's sin.[3] This, too, may be what Paul is doing in 1 Thessalonians 5:19–20. Whatever the case, at one time or another we all quench the Spirit either knowingly or unknowingly. And when we do, God often uses a human counselor or counselors. Larry Crabb has said:

> Because of our commitment to remain in control of our world for purposes of self-protection, we are unwilling to experience our desperate pain and to repent of our sinful strategies. It is therefore true that no one sees

himself clearly until he is exposed by another. God has provided three instruments to promote self-exposure: The Word of God (Heb. 4:12–13), the Spirit of God (Ps. 139:23–24), and the People of God (Heb. 3:13).[4]

There are times when "we are simply not aware of all that we are doing in our deceitful hearts."[5] But that does not mean that we are unable to determine what our thoughts, feelings, and motives really are. First Corinthians 2:15–16 says:

> He who is spiritual appraises all things, yet he himself is appraised by no man. For who has known the mind of the Lord, that he should instruct Him. But we have the mind of Christ.

Paul says here that he who is spiritual can discer "all things, because Christians have the mind of Christ. In the context, this is clearly a reference to the Spirit's work in the believer's life. God has given us His Spirit "that we might know the things freely given to us by God" (1 Cor. 2:12).

One can be fully aware of what one feels and thinks and what motivates one if one is willing to allow the Holy Spirit and God's Word to inform one. But sometimes Christians are not willing. The problem is that we sometimes consciously choose not to trust God and let Him help us deal with our thoughts, feelings, and motives. When we are disappointed or disillusioned with Him for whatever reason, we often choose a sinful course of action, and in the process we quench the Spirit. It is at this point that we need the help of fellow believers to expose our unbelief, sinful strategies, and to encourage us to trust God more fully. This is why the writer of Hebrews commands us all to "encourage one another day after day, as long as it is still called 'Today,' lest any one of you be hardened by the deceitfulness of sin" (Heb. 3:13).

There is the ever-present danger, even among the "brethren" of sin hardening us toward God and His truth. So we need to encourage one another to trust Him. And if a fellow believer refuses to do so, we must encourage that one to admit his or her sin of unbelief (3:12) and the reasons behind it.

Human counselors are needed when we refuse to do what we know is right or when we will not admit that sin is hardening us. But we also need human counselors when we are ignorant about some aspect of God's Word. Proverbs 11:14 reminds us that "where there is no guidance, the people fall, but in abundance of counselors there is victory."

All of us at times need counsel from someone who either knows the Bible a little better than we do, or someone who can help us specifically apply what we already know. While it is true that the Spirit ultimately teaches us all things (John 14:26) and guides us into all truth (John 16:13), God has chosen to use human helpers in this process as well. It is not because God could not do it all Himself. As in the process of salvation, God could draw people to Himself without any human instrument; yet He has sovereignly chosen to use people like you and me to lead others to a saving knowledge of Jesus Christ (Acts 1:8).

In God's overall plan for helping hurting believers and moving them toward maturity, He has decided to use His Spirit, His Word, and human counselors. Even though God's Word does not explicitly command the church to counsel, nor does it use *counsel* in the modern sense of the word, the Bible does command us to do what counselors do and to allow ourselves to be counseled when we need it.

When counseling *is* enough

Galatians 6:1 commands Christians who are spiritual to restore fellow believers who are trapped in sin. The term *spiritual* refers to believers who are both mature enough to recognize when another is caught in sin and mature enough to know how to help that one. This obviously rules out some people. But the command applies to many others. God is commanding spiritually mature Christians to help restore believers who are struggling with sin. This will involve exhortation and encouragement, which, in a word, is *counseling*. On the flip side, this also means that those who are caught in sin need to be willing to be counseled. Since God is commanding some to restore, He is also commanding those who need restoration to allow others to help restore them.

In the very next verse God also commands believers to bear one another's burdens. The word *burden* in this verse refers to "the excess burdens which we need to share with one another, in contrast to the load (different Greek word), in verse 5 which means the normal amount each must carry for himself."[6] Clearly the word *burden* here is not referring to sin. That issue was addressed in verse 1. Christians who are caught in sin need to be restored, which involves counseling. But people who are carrying a burden need fellow Christians to help them bear up under it. The sinning one needs exhortation and encouragement to do what is right. The one who is carrying a burden needs comfort and help.

You may be carrying a burden—a burden because you have been sinned against. This is certainly the case when an eight-year-old girl is the victim of incest. In this situation, comfort and help is going to be needed to lift her burden, and this clearly involves counseling.

In other cases, a person is burdened with difficult circumstances: perhaps cancer, a job layoff, or the loss of a loved one. Once again, words of comfort and encouragement, and, in some instances, physical help will be needed to ease these tremendous burdens. And when one attempts to comfort and encourage another, that is counseling.

So, God's Word commands us to counsel those who are sinning and to counsel those who have been sinned against or who are struggling under adverse circumstances. The word *counsel* is not used, but that is at least a part of what is being commanded. We should be willing to counsel fellow believers and to heed wise counsel from fellow believers.

Counseling: good reasons and bad

Now I realize that Galatians 6:1–2 does not mandate professional counselors, and that it is clear that much of the counseling ministry in the body of Christ can and should be done by laypeople in informal settings. A lot more Christian counseling inside and outside of the local church should be done by spiritually mature laypeople. Having said that, there is no reason to conclude that God is opposed to professional Christian counselors. There are situations that require more time, Bible knowledge, and experience than even the most mature layperson possesses. This is why professional counselors, whether pastors or Christian counselors outside the local church, are necessary at times. Just because counselors are not explicitly mentioned in the Bible does not mean that they are unbiblical. The Bible does not mention church buildings, Christian Education directors, or Sunday schools. But these facilities, people, and ministries have proved invaluable to the cause of Christ and serve a biblical function. That is what counts.

As much as possible, laypeople in local churches need to counsel one another in obedience to Galatians 6:1–2. But when no one is willing or able to counsel those who are struggling with sin, the consequences of another's sin, or the effects of living in a fallen world, then it is wise to seek out a professional Christian counselor. The next chapter is a guide to finding a counselor. But before that issue is discussed, it is important to point out a legitimate concern with regard to counseling.

Sometimes I talk to Christians who have been going to weekly or regular counseling sessions for three, five, even ten years. It conjures up images for me of non-Christians who boast that they have been in analysis for years. I also know that some believers object to counseling because they feel that it fosters a dependence upon a mortal person rather than the living God. I understand this concern and I share it. Even though God uses human helpers like counselors, the ultimate goal of counseling should be to point people toward God and to encourage a greater dependence upon Him, not just to solve problems. As we mature as believers we bring greater glory to God, and as we grow in our knowledge of who God is, our problems are either taken care of or we experience joy in spite of them.

There is also the danger of using counseling as a salve, crutch, or Band-Aid, when it should equip us to live life for God and motivate us to know Him better. If you continue to go for counseling and you are not growing as a Christian and in your knowledge of God, you are not really getting well. You may feel better right now, but you will not be better in the long run. God does not intend for counseling to be the end, but merely a means to the end, which is Himself (John 17:3).

Summary

Even if you have found a counselor that you like, if you cannot honestly say that you are making progress toward Christian maturity and knowing God better, then you need to find a different counselor.

If you have been going to a Christian counselor steadily for years and your dependence upon God has not steadily increased, then you should look for someone else who will help you to find God.

How does a person begin to find a different counselor—especially if one has already gone for counseling, perhaps more than once, and it didn't really help? That's the subject of the next chapter.

Questions for Reflection and Action

1. Do you understand the biblical basis for counseling and the two basic reasons why almost all Christians require counsel at some point in their lives?

2. Are you carrying a burden that needs to be shared with a spiritually mature Christian or counselor? If so, are you willing to let someone help you with it?

3. Have you been going regularly to a counselor for over a year? If so, do you think that you have experienced significant growth as a person and as a Christian? Are you getting to know God well and depending on Him more than on human counselors?

4. If your answer is no to the last two questions, have you considered finding a new counselor? If so, do you think that you have a good idea of how to look for one?

Notes

[1]D. Edmond Hiebert, *The Thessalonian Epistle.* Chicago: Moody Press, 1971, p. 243.

[2]Ibid. See pp. 243–245 for a fuller discussion of this issue.

[3]See pages 24–25 in the author's book, *Why Christians Sin,* for a further discussion of this truth.

[4]Larry Crabb, *Understanding People.* Grand Rapids, MI: Zondervan, 1987, p. 146.

[5]Ibid., p. 146.

[6]Charles Ryrie, *Ryrie Study Bible* (NIV). Chicago: Moody Press, 1986, p. 1777.

11. Finding A Counselor

A WOMAN I know well has struggled for years with a host of personal problems. She has been severely abused by relatives, rejected by her husband, plagued by strong feelings of worthlessness and guilt, and oppressed by satanic lies and deceptions. Much of her life she has been totally miserable, even though she has sought professional help from many sources. In each case she felt that she was either overly medicated, misunderstood, or simply not cared for. In short, she did not feel helped. But in all this she never came to see me, her pastor, or any other pastor. Finally, a concerned friend insisted that she pay me a visit, and actually came with her.

When I heard this woman's story, my heart ached, but when I realized that she had been attending our church for years and never asked for help, I felt even worse. I could have helped her or referred her to someone who could have addressed her problems in an effective and caring manner. But it never occurred to her to contact me. Now she is linked up with a number of people who are helping her, but I wish that she could have gotten what she needed years ago.

In the past, most people experiencing personal problems went to their minister, rabbi, or priest before anyone else. Today some people still do, but many try to find help on their own. They look in the Yellow Pages, ask a friend for a recommendation, or call a government agency. Sometimes these hurting people find the help they need, but in many cases they go from counselor to counselor looking for the right one. Instead of this trial and error approach, I recommend meeting with your pastor first, for the following reasons.

First of all, your pastor may be just the counselor that you need. Not all pastors are competent and caring counselors, and those who are are often in demand. Your pastor may not be willing or able to counsel you, but it is something that you should consider and pursue with him.

I find that many evangelical pastors understand God's Word well and care deeply about the needs of others. But even this is not enough to effectively counsel people unless they also have a well-thought out approach to counseling based on Scripture. Before counseling with your pastor you may want to ask him to explain his philosophy and goals for counseling. You may also want to have him discuss how he would handle problems, such as depression or self-esteem. If he dismisses your inquiry or does not seem to know exactly where he is going, then maybe he is not the best person to counsel you.

If your pastor knows Scripture well, but does not know how to specifically apply it to people's lives, then this is also a problem. The way he preaches should give you a strong indication of his ability to apply God's Word. If in the pulpit he explains the Bible plainly and then brings it together in practical, relevant principles that can be applied in life, then he will probably do the same in counseling. But a pastor who knows God's Word but cannot or will not put it into understandable, relevant principles is not going to be helpful.

Whether your pastor is not qualified to counsel you or he is already too busy helping others, he is still often in the best position to refer you to someone who can help. Pastors are usually privy to information about particular counselors that the average lay person is not. Your pastor probably knows which counselors in your area have actually helped other people in your congregation. He may also be aware of the theological and philosophical bent of certain counselors, and therefore can steer you away from people who are dangerous or deceptive.

Case in point. A few years ago a woman from our church came to my office to let me know that she planned to meet with a counselor new to our community. I don't think that she had come to seek my approval or advice, she simply wanted to let me know what she was going to do. Nevertheless, I asked her if she would mind telling me with whom she was going to counsel. She said she didn't mind and told me his name. The name set off an alarm in me and I asked, "Do you realize that this counselor is a Mormon?" The look on her face said I could have knocked her over with a feather. She had no knowledge of his religious affiliation. He simply advertised himself as a "Christian counselor" and she assumed that he must be an evangelical Christian. In my experience, it is not unusual for many types of counselors to label themselves as "Christian." Just because one says that one is, doesn't make it so. This is the second reason why I believe that people should check with their pastors about possible counselors, and I am not alone in this conviction.

In a paid advertisement in *Christianity Today* entitled "How To Choose A Counselor," sponsored by the American Association of Christian Counselors, there is a section about "finding the right counselor." The first step given is to "ask for referrals: Requesting recommendations from a pastor or trusted friend . . . ."[1] Christian counseling professionals also realize that your pastor is often the best person to consult when beginning the search for a counselor.

Tim Jackson, in his booklet, *When Help Is Needed,* says,

> In a best-case situation, your pastor will refer you to a lay counselor in the church or to a professional, and then check with you from time to time to see if your needs for counsel are being met. It is just as important that you be sure the help you are getting is consistent with biblical values, Christ-centered faith, and godly pastoral oversight.[2]

As Jackson indicates, it is wise to get a referral from your pastor, but it is also important to keep him informed and to get his input during the entire counseling process. Sometimes this is not possible or desirable, but usually it is helpful. Your pastor is, one hopes, a shepherd who cares about your overall well-being, and ultimately he has the responsibility for ministering to you after your counseling is over. What's more, he is probably in the best position to get you into a good discipleship relationship.

As pointed out earlier in this book, what is often needed, along with wise counsel, is discipling. Even if a hurting person receives proper counseling, that counsel needs to be accompanied by or followed up with personal or small group discipleship. Normally this should be done through a local church with pastoral oversight and direction. Your pastor will often be the one who helps you get set up in a discipleship situation where you can continue to progress toward maturity and wholeness. The need for discipleship should be discussed and established from the very beginning of the counseling process. Sometimes this can happen without pastoral involvement, but usually he is the one who arranges for this important aspect of the healing process.

Having recommended pastoral involvement or referral, when appropriate and necessary, what if a person has already pursued this avenue and for whatever reason it has not worked out? Where does one then go to find a new counselor?

Where do I go from here?

There are reputable Christian organizations and counseling ministries that offer help in finding a counselor. For instance, the Institute for Biblical Counseling, associated with Colorado Christian College, will refer callers to its graduates. If one calls the school (303) 697-5425 and gives one's geographical location, the caller will be given the name and telephone number of the nearest practicing counselor.

Focus on the Family also has a counselor referral service (719) 531-3400. If one calls and asks for a referral, one will be given the name and number of a Christian counselor nearby. These counselors are not a part of the Focus on the Family organization; they have simply asked to be included in the counselor referral directory. Each one has been checked out, to a certain extent, by the Focus on the Family ministry.

Some Christian counseling and recovery clinics have hotlines that can be called for a referral. For example, the Rapha clinics have just such a hotline (800) 383-HOPE. Here, too, people can be referred to counselors in their city or geographical area who are recommended by this Christian recovery ministry.

Sometimes there are published directories of Christian counselors such as the one provided in *Christianity Today* (May 17, 1993). As with many counselor directories, there is no guarantee about the quality of the counselors listed,[3] and this is certainly the case when one simply picks a counselor out of the Yellow Pages.

How can I know for sure?

How can a person be sure that a new counselor will be any different or better than the last? There is no way to be absolutely sure. But to find the best counselor for you, you must be willing to take an active, assertive part in selecting one. A person has to ask questions before beginning the counseling process and these questions have to be the right ones. No matter who recommends a counselor or how reputable an organization that counselor is with, you have to check the person out yourself. Following is a list of questions I believe a person should ask any prospective counselor before making a commitment for counseling:

1. "Tell me what your understanding of the gospel is and how you came to trust Christ as your Savior."

As has been discussed, there are counselors who call themselves "Christian," but truly are not. Listen carefully to the counselor's testimony. Is the person trusting in Christ alone for forgiveness of sins or is he or she also depending upon some form of good works as well? If the counselor is trusting in Christ plus good works, this person is not truly saved (see Eph. 2:8–9) and this error will affect his or her counseling adversely.

2. "Is the goal of counsel to make me healthy or is its goal to make me godly?"[4]

There is definitely a sense in which God wants us to be spiritually and emotionally healthy. In fact, that is one reason why Christ went to the cross, so that you and I could be healed (1 Peter 2:24). Nevertheless, this is a by-product of knowing Christ as Savior and growing into His likeness. *The primary goal of counseling should be godliness and Christian maturity.* Then we will experience personal wholeness and the abundant life that Christ promised and for which we long. Make sure that your counselor has all this in the right order.

3. "What is your view of Scripture and how do you use it in counseling?"

Does the counselor see Scripture as the final inerrant authority in regard to truth? Is his or her counsel "guided" by Scripture or merely "tested" against it? Does he or she start with Scriptural principles and then build on that with proven psychological insights or does he or she basically depend on psychological principles and then go looking for Scripture to support his or her presuppositions? How specific will he or she get in applying Scriptural principles? This is a crucial question. Keep asking probing questions until you are satisfied that his or her counsel will ultimately be based on God's unchanging Word, rather than the shifting sand of psychological studies.

4. "What is sin and to what extent is it involved in personal problems?"

It is important to know that your counselor definitely sees certain thoughts and behaviors as being morally wrong. But equally important is his or her definition of sin. Are only those things sin explicitly listed in Scripture as morally wrong? Or is anything contrary to God's character and purposes sin? Beyond this is the question of how sin is involved in our personal problems. Tim Jackson so accurately states that,

Counseling is dangerous if it treats us as people whose hearts are full of motives that are either all good or all bad. It is dangerous if it leaves us feeling as though none of our thoughts or emotions are legitimate. It is also dangerous if it treats us as basically good people who have had more than our share of bad breaks. Counsel needs to help us see the difference between legitimate, God-given desires and our own foolish attempts to satisfy those desires. Good guidance must help us to sort out the dignity of desires that reflect our creation in the likeness of God and those twisted strategies that reflect the depravity of our fall into sin.[5]

If a counselor sees personal problems exclusively and totally as a result of sin, look elsewhere. But if your prospective counselor feels that sin often has little or no part in people's problems, then I also advise you to keep searching.

5. *"What is your view of God, and specifically, is He both all-loving and all-powerful?"*

How a counselor views God makes all the difference in the world in terms of his or her counseling. Does the counselor believe that God is a personal God who knows and cares about every aspect of our lives? Is God an all-powerful God who ultimately "causes all things to work together for good" (Rom. 8:28) "according to the counsel of His will" (Eph. 1:11, NKJV)? If God is not all-loving and all-powerful, then He is too imperfect and small a God to trust. Make sure that your counselor has a big God! In other words, the God of the Bible.

6. *"Are you willing to actively cooperate with other professionals if I give you permission to do so?"*

Some counselors feel that they are so uniquely qualified to help people that they refuse to cooperate with other professionals, such as medical doctors, pastors, and therapists. I would be wary of any counselor who expresses a reluctance to work with others, especially if you desire your doctor or pastor to be informed and consulted throughout the counseling process. If this is your desire (and I believe it should be), express it to your prospective counselor and offer to sign all necessary release forms if and when counseling begins.

7. "What kind of formal counseling training have you received and where did you receive it?"

Degrees, licenses, and certifications should be displayed somewhere in the office, but these may not be much help to you without a verbal explanation. If the schools or associations mentioned by the counselor are not familiar to you, you may need to do some homework on them. Generally speaking, a counselor should have at least a master's level training in counseling from an accredited school, seminary, or university.[6]

These questions may seem too intense or extensive to you, and I'm sure that some counselors will feel the same way. But this interview process is important, particularly if you have had difficulty in the past finding the right counselor. Some prospective counselors may try to dismiss these questions or act like you are out of line for asking them. But I agree with Tim Jackson, a licensed counselor, who says,

> A counselor who is unwilling to answer questions concerning his own values, and the approach he uses, is not worthy of your time or money. Reputable counselors should have some kind of printed disclosure statement that explains their training and how they view the whole counseling process. It's impossible to separate the counselor from his counseling. The two are inextricably

bound together. His philosophy of growth and change comes out of his personal theology of life. How does he view and define the problem of sin? How does he describe the process of change? Be a responsible consumer. After all, you are paying for this professional's help.[7]

I know many counselors who are more than willing to answer questions, and in fact, several I have talked to welcome such inquiries. The point is that your counselor should be as open with you as he or she desires you to be. That's only fair, and positive change can come out of such a relationship.

Now the question some of you may still have is, "What if I cannot find a good Christian counselor in my area?" This unfortunately is a very real possibility. Gary Collins acknowledges this when he says, "Frequently it simply is not possible to find a competent Christian counselor."[8] When it comes right down to it there are probably not an abundance of Christian counselors who are professionally competent, but also know and use Scripture properly in their counseling. And if a person lives well outside of a major metropolitan center, it may be difficult, if not impossible to find a good Christian counselor nearby. If this is the case for you, what steps should you take? Should you consider going to a secular counselor?

Some Christian counseling professionals believe that secular counselors can be very effectively used by God and may in fact be the "persons . . . who can best give help in times of need."[9] On the other side are Christian counseling professionals who claim that pastors should handle almost all Christian counseling and just occasionally refer counselees to "other more competent Christian workers."[10] I hold a position between these two extremes.

A Christian could or should consider going to a secular counselor if, 1) there is not a Christian counselor to be found;

2) it is a crisis situation requiring immediate help, such as a suicide attempt; 3) the secular counselor is not openly hostile to the Christian faith and, in fact, accepts the importance and validity of faith; or 4) the secular counselor provides a necessary element such as medical care and expertise that cannot be provided by a pastor or lay counselor.

Having said this, a secular counselor cannot ultimately provide what Christians need for complete healing or real growth. A secular counselor can deal with emotional issues and can even address behavioral problems in practical ways. Nevertheless, as pointed out earlier, any human problem that is emotional in nature is also spiritual in nature. The two cannot be separated. A secular counselor simply cannot address the spiritual element inherent in human problems. Even if the secular counselor gives practical advice on changing destructive behavioral patterns, he or she still cannot help believers to know Christ better. Without addressing our relationship to Christ on a deep level, only superficial or temporary growth can occur in the life of a Christian. The bottom line is that a Christian may start the process of healing and growth with a secular counselor, but at some point that believer is going to have to have a biblical counselor who ultimately encourages a closer walk with Christ. But once again, what if there is not a competent Christian counselor nearby?

It is a fact that many Christian people live in places like Muleshoe, Texas (population: 4,571), Danville, Iowa (population: 950), Eagle, Alaska (population: 250), and Lustre, Montana (population: 2). As wonderful as life may be in these locales, if for some reason life becomes extremely difficult, there may be no Christian counselors close by. I have personally checked out the availability of Christian counselors in areas like these, and I can report that if you live in a rural or remote area of the United States, you are probably a long way from a Christian counselor or clinic. Unfortunately, Christian counseling is not readily available to many Christians. But there is another important issue: money.

Most Christian counselors have to make a living and charge a fee similar if not equal to secular counselors. Even if sliding fee schedule is used to determine cost, it may not slide far enough to enable struggling Christians to receive counseling. So, if Christian counseling is a long way off and if one does not have money in the budget for it, what should a hurting Christian do?

There is no clear-cut answer here. The Bible does not give us specific help in regard to this particular question. In these situations a person needs wise counsel simply to determine whether or not to pursue counsel. That is in fact what this chapter and the previous ones are intended to provide. With that in mind, my advice would be for a hurting Christian to seek counsel from as many trustworthy people as possible (Prov. 11:14). Often a clear consensus will emerge from this. If this does not happen, the biblical principle indicated by Paul in 1 Thessalonians 3:1 comes into play.

> When we could endure it no longer, we thought it best
> to be left behind at Athens alone.

When the Bible is not explicit and wise counsel is evenly divided, Christians have to decide what they believe is the best thing to do in a given situation based on very concrete considerations (1 Thess. 3:2–5). Obviously, sincere and fervent prayer for wisdom is a part of this process (James 1:5–8), but here are some other practical and important factors as well. Consider the following questions:

1) Is your situation truly to the point where you can "endure it no longer"?

2) Have you interviewed a Christian counselor that you believe is the best person to help you?

3) Is distance going to keep you from meeting regularly with this counselor for as many times as necessary?

4) Is the money that will have to be spent going to put an even greater burden on you?

5) Can you publicly say with conviction that what you are planning to do is God's will?

Depending on your answers to these questions you may decide that it is best to pursue counseling, even though the counselor is far away and you do not have the money to pay for his or her help. There are times when this is the best thing to do.

Some time ago a severely depressed man who felt he had totally failed his family came to me with a question: "What can I do to make this up to my kids?" I told him, "The best thing you can do for them is to get your life turned around." So, even though he didn't have any money and the help he needed was eight hundred miles away, he went for it. It took a long time and cost a lot of money, but he did get his life turned around and it was the best thing he could have ever done for his family, for himself, and for the Lord.

But what about the struggling Christian who decides that counseling is not a viable or appropriate option? Is there any hope for this person? Listen to the comforting, hopeful words of Isaiah 40:28–31.

> Do you not know? Have you not heard? The Everlasting God, the Lord, the Creator of the ends of the earth does not become weary or tired. He gives strength to the weary, and to him who lacks might He increases power. Though youths grow weary and tired, and vigorous young men stumble badly, yet those who wait for the Lord will gain new strength; they will mount up with

wings like eagles, they will run and not get tired, they
will walk and not become weary.

There are times, such as when the people of Judah were
in captivity, that no human help was available for God's people. At these times we must wait for the Lord. This word does
not rule out all effort on our part, but it does mean "to wait or
to look for with eager expectation."[11] In other words, when
there is no effective human help available to us, we have to
accept that God has allowed this to be, but also that He will
provide the help we need in His time and way. We must not
despair, God is fully aware of our situation (Isa. 40:27), and
He does plan to help us! God's provision begins when we
truly decide to wait for the Lord. Then our weakness is
exchanged for His strength.

This is what Isaiah means when he says, "Those who
wait for the LORD will gain new strength; they will mount up
with wings like eagles, they will run and not get tired, they
will walk and not become weary." When one puts one's trust
in God, one will find in Him the strength and endurance that
one needs for the trials of life. Sometimes, in line with His
wise and loving purposes, God decides it is best for us that
our problems remain,[12] and he gives us the strength we need
to endure them, supernatural strength.[13]

Amy Carmichael was a missionary to India for fifty-six
years. During the last twenty years, however, she was confined to her room because of injuries suffered as a result of a
terrible fall. In spite of being daily wracked by pain, she carried on her work for the Lord and composed thirteen books.

In 1948, as she neared the end of her life, Amy wrote
this note: "Not relief from pain, not relief from the weariness
that follows, not anything of that sort at all, is my chief need.
Thou, O Lord my God, are my need—Thy courage, Thy
patience, Thy fortitude. And very much I need a quickened
gratitude for the countless helps given every day."[14]

If you find yourself far from help or you recognize that you cannot afford it or you simply cannot locate anyone suitable to help you at any price or distance, you must wait for the Lord. Down through the centuries many precious saints have had to do just this and God has faithfully supplied strength for them. He can and will do it again for you, if you trust Him.

Notes

[1]*Christianity Today,* May 17, 1993, pp. 58–59.
[2]Tim Jackson, *When Help Is Needed.* Grand Rapids, MI: Radio Bible Class, 1992, p. 26.
[3]*Christianity Today,* May 17, 1993, p. 60.
[4]Tim Jackson, p. 18
[5]Tim Jackson, p. 16.
[6]See the article, "How To Choose A Counselor," *Christianity Today,* May 17, 1993, p. 59 for additional input regarding a counselor's professional training.
[7]Tim Jackson, p. 28.
[8]Gary Collins, *Can You Trust Psychology?* Downers Grove, IL: InterVarsity Press, 1988, p. 32.
[9]Gary Collins, p. 33.
[10]Jay Adams, *Competent To Counsel.* Grand Rapids, MI: Baker, 1970, p. 18.
[11]R. Laird Harris, Gleason L. Archer, Jr., Bruce K. Waltke, *Theological Workbook of the Old Testament.* Chicago: Moody Press, 1980, p. 791.
[12]See 2 Corinthians 12:7–10 for a real-life example of this truth. Whatever was Paul's "thorn in the flesh," it was a real problem for him and yet God decided it would remain.
[13]I am indebted to Haddon Robinson for this understanding of Isaiah 40:31.
[14]Elisabeth Elliot, *A Chance To Die.* Old Tappan, NJ: Revell, 1987, p. 365.

Part 2

12. Depression

Down in the dumps I'll never go,
That's where the devil keeps me low,
So I'll sing with all my might,
And I'll keep my armor bright,
But, down in the dumps I'll never go.
—Author unknown

LEHMAN Strauss, Bible teacher and conference speaker, says in his book, *In God's Waiting Room,* that he used to sing this little chorus often. After his wife's fatal stroke, however, he admits that he landed in the "dumps" for quite a while.[1]

Many great men and women of God have struggled with depression, including C. H. Spurgeon[2] and J. B. Phillips,[3] just to name two. Depression is the most common problem counselors confront today.[4] I say this not to minimize depression nor to excuse it, but rather to point out that there should be no shame in being depressed. Even mature Christians can and do become depressed. It is unfortunate, however, when a person continues to wrestle with depression primarily because one is unwilling to admit one is depressed and to seek help.

Many Christians experience intense and/or prolonged bouts of depression. Some of these believers are very open about their struggle and are not hesitant to seek help and counsel. Others still believe that "good" Christians never get depressed, or at least not for long. These believers not only have to try to deal with their depression, they must also deal with the additional feelings of guilt about the way they are failing God, themselves, and others.

A good friend of our family began feeling depressed a few years ago. But since she thought that Christians should not get depressed, she refused to admit it for over a year. Finally things reached the point where she had to see a medical doctor about severe physical symptoms. As it turned out, the root cause of her depression was probably organic, but as is usually the case, there were other significant spiritual/emotional factors as well. The worst aspect of her depression was the guilt that she was carrying. This woman was overwhelmed by the feeling that she had horribly failed her husband, her family, and her God. Happily, with medication, biblical counsel, and an understanding and supportive husband, she is making significant progress.

Probably the biggest reason why many Christians continue to battle depression is that they are ashamed to admit it and get help. But what about those who have sought help, perhaps diligently, and yet are not doing significantly better? And what about those who have gone to pastors or a Christian psychologists or psychiatrists and have tried to deal with their problems, but the feelings of depression are still there, perhaps worse than ever? Is there any hope for these people? The answer is a most emphatic *yes*! Hope is precisely what depressed people need, and it is what they must have to overcome their depression, because depression at its very roots is hopelessness.

Frank Minirth and Walter Byrd state that 75 percent of depressives feel they will "never get better."[5] While I do not disagree with their assessment, I would take it a step further and state that all depressed people struggle to a great extent with hopelessness over their situation. Depression *is* the loss of hope.

Elijah was a great man of God. He was one of the greatest prophets of Old Testament times. And yet he fell into a very serious depression. He didn't just get "the blues," nor was he simply discouraged. Elijah was depressed. After the wonderful display of God's power on Mt. Carmel and the tremendous victory over the prophets of Baal (1 Kings 18), Elijah became severely depressed. Apparently he thought that after these events the people of Israel would rise up against the evil King Ahab and that Jezebel would react like a frightened puppy. However, when the people of Israel did not act and Jezebel did, Elijah concluded that things were hopeless. He had done all that he could. He had given it his best shot and failed. If after all this the situation was still the same, then things were truly hopeless. In this state of depression, Elijah lost the desire to live, he slept excessively, and he had to be encouraged to eat (19:1–6).

Some Christians lose hope of ever being loved again. Others lose hope of ever being gainfully employed. Still others feel that the situation with their rebellious child is hopeless. Some depressed believers do not know why they are depressed, but they feel hopeless about ever feeling better. Whatever the particular reason for the loss of hope, the need for hope is the common denominator among all depressed people. This is why when I begin to counsel a depressed person, I always say up front that he or she will get better, or that things will get better. I always try to give hope.

Now someone may say at this point, "You can't assure a depressed person that he or she will get better. What if he or she doesn't?" My point is that without hope one can't get better. Loss of hope is his or her most basic problem.

Don Baker was a very successful pastor who became severely depressed. He was even hospitalized for his depression. Shortly after he was admitted, a counselor came by to visit with him. The counselor asked a number of probing questions and then finished with these hopeful words, "You are deeply depressed—you do need help—you do need to be here—but you'll get better. It will take time, but you'll get better."[6] Baker said later,

> I'll always be grateful for those gentle words—
> profound in their simplicity—yet filled with hope. And
> oh, how I needed hope . . . . Over and over again during
> those uncertain and confusing days, I thanked my Lord
> for a wise and thoughtful counselor who had taken time
> to give me hope.[7]

When I tell family members and counselors that they should give hope to the depressed person, I am not saying that we should give false hope. One cannot, for instance, tell a person who is depressed because he or she has cancer that the cancer will go into remission. No one but God knows such things. Nor should one assure a depressed person that he or she will be feeling better within a certain time frame. But one can state with certainty that in time and with proper help the depression will lift. This is particularly true for the Christian because God is at work in our lives (Phil. 2:13). We can be sure that He is working all things for "the good," including a person's depression (Rom. 8:28).

David was probably depressed when he wrote Psalm 42. He says that "my tears have been my food day and night, while they continually say to me 'Where is your God?' " (42:3). But he goes on to say, "Why are you cast down, O my soul? And why are you disquieted within me? Hope in God, for I shall yet praise Him for the help of His countenance" (42:5).

Another major reason why Christians who have sought counseling still continue in depression has to do with physical problems. John White, a Christian psychiatrist, states in his book, *The Masks of Melancholy,* that "while doctors frequently refer depressed Christians to me, pastoral counselors rarely do so."[8] Many pastors and some Christian counselors apparently still believe that depression is always caused by spiritual/emotional problems. This is unfortunate, because although this is often the case, it isn't necessarily so. Some depression starts with physiological problems. Gary Collins points to a study that indicates that perhaps 40 percent of all depression cases can be linked to physical illness.[9]

For instance, bipolar depression is a hereditary physical disorder that has to be treated with medication for as long as the affected person lives. Counseling alone will have little or no effect on these depressed individuals. There are other problems like seasonal affective disorder which plagues people who do not receive sufficient sunlight for prolonged periods of time. Once again, counseling may be a part of the treatment, but only a part. This is why anyone who counsels a depressed individual should insist that he or she see a doctor at some point in the counseling process. I usually insist that depressed people see a doctor at the very onset of counseling. If there is a physical cause or physical problem contributing to the depression, it needs to be treated. Even the wisest, most biblical counselor will not be enough for these individuals.

On the other hand, there are Christian medical professionals who apparently believe that most depressions are caused by chemical imbalances. Anti-depressants are prescribed too frequently and for too long. It is true that a few people have to continue on antidepressants for life. It is also true that even if a depression began with spiritual/emotional problem, eventually the depression can become a physical one. This is commonly known as "clinical depression." In this situation the depressed individual needs anti-depressants in order to get well more quickly and to deal with the root causes of depression. But, as Minirth and Byrd point out,

> The basic [spiritual/emotional] problems must still be dealt with in order to really help the patient. The medications serve to help the patient become mentally functional through balancing the biochemistry of the brain so that the patient can then progress in therapy.[10]

In other words, medication alone cannot fully cure most depressed people. In order for the depressed Christian to be whole again, he or she must have biblical counsel that helps to correct both wrong thought and wrong behavior patterns.

When medication *and* counseling aren't enough

What about depressed believers who have had proper medication and good counsel and yet they are still depressed?

Remember Elijah? In order to help him out of his depression, God exhorted him to eat (1 Kings 19:5), questioned his behavior and thinking (19:8), and sent him on a special assignment to show him that he was not alone in standing for what was right (19:15–18). But, even this would not have been enough to lift Elijah out of his depression. Elijah needed a fresh encounter with the true and living God.

As discussed earlier, when one is depressed, it means that he or she feels hopeless. In many cases, whether it is admitted or not, the depressed believer is disappointed or disillusioned with God. One thinks—incorrectly—that God has let one down. The depressed Christian either believes that God is not powerful enough to help or that God simply does not care. When this is the case, all the medication and counseling in the world will not be enough. The disillusioned believer will have to have a fresh encounter with God.

In Elijah's case, it happened on the same mountain where God appeared to Moses in the burning bush.[11] First, God gave Elijah a reminder of His incredible power by sending a strong wind, an earthquake, and fire to impress him with His might. God wanted Elijah to realize anew that nothing was too difficult for Him (Jer. 32:27). Therefore, he could yet hope for God to change things.

Then, after this tremendous display of power, God spoke to Elijah in a "still, small voice" (1 Kings 19:12) and gently said to him again, "What are you doing here, Elijah?" (19:13). God wanted Elijah to recognize afresh that He is not just powerful, but personal as well. He cares intensely about His people, and not just His people as a whole, but every person who puts his or her faith in God. Elijah could have hope because God was not only powerful, but He cared about him individually.

The point is that medication, proper diet, exercise, and counseling are all important and good for the depressed Christian. But in some cases, perhaps many, the depressed believer is going to have to see God as He really is—again. God has to break in to the life of the depressed believer and show him or her who He is again and that there is a reason for hope. Until this happens, there can be some improvement and progress, but complete wholeness cannot be achieved until the depressed individual meets with God.

Sometimes the depressed Christian encounters God gradually through the process of discipling. As one digs deeper into God's Word, one hears God speaking. As one pours out one's heart to God in prayer, he or she senses God's affirming presence. As one fellowships with other believers, one sees Christ reaching out to him or her through them. As a result of these quiet encounters, one may begin to have real hope. In other cases, the encounter with God can be quite direct, as it was with Elijah.

A man I know well had been depressed about a personal tragedy for some time. His wife had been changed by a stroke from a healthy, vibrant woman into a person who was unable to do many of the things she used to do. This was very frustrating for both of them. Their lives and lifestyle were radically changed overnight. It was a very difficult adjustment, and continues to be. But it was a lot tougher before God broke in.

One night when he was particularly depressed about the situation and was about to give up on everyone and everything, God turned on the light for him. The man says "it just hit me" that God really cares about my wife and me and He has a good and loving plan that He is working in our lives. He had an encounter with the living God and truths that he already knew he truly embraced as if for the first time. And for the first time in a long time, he had hope. Real hope.

When one encounters God afresh, that does not necessarily mean that one will immediately be whole again. However, that encounter can be the turning point. At that point the depressed person should be willing to think and act correctly, but the pilgrimage to wholeness is often not complete for a while.

After his dramatic meeting with God, Elijah was not completely out of his depression. His verbal response to God was no different than before (19:14). Yet, he was willing to go anoint two new kings and a prophet who would work along side him and eventually succeed him (19:15–21). It is interesting that after Elijah's anointing of Elisha, we do not read about him again until Ahab steals Naboth's vineyard. One cannot be dogmatic, but apparently Elijah continued to recover from his depression for some time after his meeting with God. But his encounter was what really started him on the road to recovery.

Summary

The bottom line for those suffering with depression is that there is hope! However, one must admit the problem and seek help for both the physical and spiritual/emotional aspects of depression. But when the problem is ultimately disappointment and disillusionment with God, the depressed Christian should not only be counseled, but also discipled. In the process of discipling, one may meet with God quietly or God may break into one's life dramatically. Although we do not know how or where the person will encounter God, it will eventually happen in God's time and in His way.

There is hope for the depressed, but that hope is not ultimately in counseling, but in God.

Notes

[1]Lehman Strauss, *In God's Waiting Room.* Chicago: Moody, 1985, p. 11.

[2]Arnold Dallimore, *Spurgeon: A New Biography.* Carlisle, PA: The Banner of Truth, 1985.

[3]Wayne Montbleau, *The Wounded Healer.* Old Tappan, NJ: Revell, 1979.

[4]Frank Minirth and Walter Byrd, *Christian Psychiatry.* Old Tappan, NJ: Revell, 1990, p. 136.

[5]Ibid., p. 133.

[6]Don Baker and Emery Nester, *Depression: Finding Hope and Meaning in Life's Darkest Shadow.* Portland, OR: Multnomah Press, 1983, pp. 23–24.

[7]Ibid., p. 24.

[8]John White, *The Masks of Melancholy.* Downers Grove, IL: InterVarsity Press, 1982, p. 77.

[9]Gary Collins, *Case Studies in Christian Counseling.* Waco, TX: Word, 1988, p. 112.

[10]Frank Minirth and Walter Byrd, p. 147.

[11]Cross reference 1 Kings 19:8 with Exodus 3:1.

13. Addiction

Shortly after I began ministering at my first church, a couple from the community was led to Christ by a seminary student in our congregation. They were both drinkers, heavy smokers, and in general, people who loved loud music and night-long parties. They knew little about Christ except how to use His name in a profane way. But, when the gospel was clearly and lovingly laid out before them, they embraced it without reservation. The change in their lives was profound and dramatic. Their whole lifestyle changed overnight in many respects.

For instance, about a week after they trusted Christ they asked the man who led them to Christ if their smoking habit was pleasing to God. He told them that smoking was not explicitly mentioned as a sin in Scripture, but that it probably violated several biblical principles, especially if it exercised any control over their lives. They admitted they were addicted to it and thus decided it was wrong. At that point, they bowed in prayer and simply asked God to take away their desire to smoke and to help them not to ever smoke again. From that moment on, these two individuals stopped smoking completely and to the best of my knowledge, have not touched a cigarette since.

I relate this event to make an important point. When people are truly born again, a transformation occurs and believers lay "aside the old self with its evil practices" (Col. 3:9). God helps Christians put aside many of the sins and sinful habits that characterized their lives before Christ, including addictions. I know of many people over the years who, when they trusted Christ, were set free from various kinds of addictions: alcohol, drugs, sex. These people were hopelessly hooked, but without any help other than God's, they kicked their habits "cold turkey." I know that God helps people in this way and I always advise Christians who have an addiction to ask God to miraculously take away this desire and give them the strength to say "no" from then on. Sometimes He does, but sometimes He doesn't.

This chapter is written especially for Christians who have asked God for this particular kind of miracle, but have not yet received it. Perhaps some have been asking for it for years. Probably most of these believers have sought counseling or have been to recovery clinics. Some have received the help they needed and are doing fine. But many Christians with addictions have been through counseling, clinics, and other programs, but realize that their addictions still have too much control over them. What went wrong? Why didn't it help enough to make the difference? And why does God miraculously remove the bondage of addiction for some and not for others?

In regard to the last question, I have to say that I do not know. I do know, however, that God has good and loving plans for all of His children (Jer. 29:11), and I believe that there is an opportunity for all Christians to rid themselves of any addiction, no matter how powerful or entrenched it may be.

Colossians 3:9 indicates that Christians have "laid aside the old self." When a person trusts Christ, many of the sins and habits of one's former lifestyle fall away. However, as Ephesians 4:22 indicates, one always has sins from one's former manner of living that still need to be put aside. I believe the verb translated "lay aside" is a timeless command.[1] It is a never ending process. Sometimes God miraculously strips away sinful habits and desires from a person's life, but He never takes them all away until we see Him face-to-face (1 John 3:2). It is the Christian's responsibility to continue stripping off sinful habits, and God has given us the resources to do so. The question is, how can we do it?

To deal effectively with an addiction, one must first believe that God is willing and able to help. In Philippians 4:13, Paul is the example in this regard when he states that "I can do all things through Him who strengthens me." The Bible says that there is nothing a believer cannot do with God's help, and this is especially true of those things God commands a believer to do. Until one is willing to fully accept this truth, one will not be able to effectively deal with one's addiction. But complete acceptance of this truth alone is not enough. If a Christian has an addiction, he or she has to be willing to confess it and to ask God to help him or her with it. This is the first reason people with addictions, including Christians, do not get control over their addictive behaviors. Many are in a state of denial.

When I talk about denial, I am not speaking of it in the same sense as the secular recovery industry does. As William Playfair correctly points out, secular counselors define denial as "the 'symptom' of chemical addiction that makes it impossible for the chemically dependent to 'recognize' their problems or admit to being addicted."[2] Rather, I am referring to denial as it is commonly practiced by all human beings since Adam, who was the first to deny he had sinned and instead blamed his wife (Gen. 3:12).

Christians are totally capable of recognizing their addictions with the help of the Holy Spirit and God's written Word. The problem is not one of recognition, but acceptance of personal responsibility. When Christians become addicted to something, perhaps not immediately, but eventually the Spirit working with the Word will convict them that it is sin (John 16:8) and that it is something for which they need to seek God's help. When addicted believers quench the Spirit, refuse to accept that they are sinning, and refuse to avail themselves of God's resources, that is denial.

But what about those who have the disease of alcoholism? What about the people who are genetically programmed to be addicted? Are we saying that these people are simply sinners who will not take responsibility for their behavior? My answer is yes and no.

There are some researchers who deny virtually any link between addiction and genetics/disease.[3] I do not have the expertise to argue with medical researchers on either side of the debate. I am willing to believe that some people may have a genetic or organic predisposition to addiction. However, I would still maintain that even if this is the case, these people are still able to do what is right. *Predisposition* does not mean *causation.* The fact is that everyone without Christ has a predisposition to sin. Yet God will hold us accountable for our actions and there will be no excuses (Rom. 1:20). *Predisposition* simply means that one has a strong desire or craving to do something. It does not mean that one has to do it. This is particularly true for Christians who have the Spirit and the Word. Thus even if one has a genetic/organic predisposition to addiction, one is still capable, with the help of God and others, of doing what is right. If a Christian refuses to accept personal responsibility and seek help for his or her addiction, that person is in denial and cannot be helped effectively.

So how does one encourage a believer in denial to accept responsibility and seek help? First, the person has to be counseled about his or her disappointment and disillusionment with God, because that is the only reason a Christian would continue in a willful state of denial.[4] The issue regarding God's character and purpose will have to be settled before the person will be willing to permanently come out of denial. However, it often helps to teach these people in denial about the difference between *legitimate* and *illegitimate* needs.

In James 4:1–3, the apostle James says,

> What is the source of quarrels and conflicts among you? Is not the source your pleasures that wage war in your members? You lust and do not have; so you commit murder. And you are envious and cannot obtain; so you fight and quarrel. You do not have because you do not ask. You ask and do not receive, because you ask with wrong motives, so that you may spend it on your pleasures.

As pointed out earlier, God has created every man and woman with certain legitimate needs. Everyone has a divinely designed need for security and significance. Ultimately we must turn to God for total fulfillment of these needs, but He also uses human relationships and earthly means to meet our needs in part.

An addicted person feels like he or she "needs" whatever he or she is addicted to, and addicted people are willing to go to great lengths to meet their needs. James indicates that some people will go as far as murder (4:1). But the need that the addicted person feels so strongly is often not a legitimate need. James says that Christians sometimes have strong cravings or desires that he calls "pleasures" (4:1, 3). These cravings are not legitimate needs, but they may feel that way. A person, for instance, may have a strong craving for alcohol, but this substance is not something that is necessary for physical or emotional health. On the contrary, it is simply for pleasure and the physical and emotional effects of alcohol are by-in-large harmful. An addicted person needs to realize that often his or her cravings are not legitimate needs. On the other hand, sometimes we desire things that are legitimate, but our motives are wrong.

In 1 Corinthians 6:12–13, the apostle Paul says,

> All things are lawful for me, but not all things are
> profitable. All things are lawful for me, but I will not be
> mastered by anything. Food is for the stomach, and the
> stomach is for food; but God will do away with both of
> them. Yet the body is not for immorality, but for the
> Lord; and the Lord is for the body.

Food is something that we all need. But when one is "mastered"—that is, controlled—by food, then the motive for eating is wrong (James 4:3). Eating becomes primarily an occasion for pleasure rather than the meeting of a need. Therefore, something like food that we all need can become an addiction if we allow it to control us for the motive of pleasure.

An addict needs to understand either that the need is illegitimate, in which case he or she must seek God's help to lay it aside, or the addicted person must see that the addiction is a legitimate need being approached in a sinful way in which he or she requires God's help to begin meeting that need appropriately. In either scenario, counseling can be used by God to give insight, which in turn can provide motivation for godly, positive change.

So, the problem of denial must be addressed first, and in a Christian this almost always goes back to disappointment or disillusionment with God. Then, the issue of whether the addiction is related to an illegitimate or legitimate need should be worked through with the addicted person. But even if one stops denying that one needs help, recognizes the source of one's addiction, and lays it aside with the help of God and others, one is still not out of danger.

Fred Smith, in his book *Learning To Lead,* shares an insight given to him by a psychiatrist.

> For a long time people couldn't understand how a man could be an alcoholic, sober up, stay sober for ten years, and then go back to drinking. Surely he knew all the problems he had as a drunk. Why go back? They found out why. People who give up alcohol but remain only abstainers can be back to drinking at any time. Those who move from abstaining to the joy of sobriety seldom return. But until they make that transition from abstaining to sobriety, they are vulnerable.[5]

This is so true. If an addict does not learn "the joy of sobriety," he or she will either lay aside one addiction and pick up another or go back to the original addiction, even after many years of abstaining. This is particularly true if the addiction is related to a legitimate, human need. Therefore, people with addictions must be taught "the joy of sobriety" and the education must continue until they have mastered it.

In Ephesians 4:22–24 Paul not only claims that believers are to "lay aside the old self," but he also says that Christians are to "put on the new self." Putting on the new self for the addict means learning to do what is right and positive (4:25–32), but it also involves learning to enjoy the Christian life and delighting one's self in the Lord.

Psalm 37:4 says, "Delight yourself in the LORD, and He will give you the desires of your heart." The addicted Christian not only needs to put aside sinful habits, but also to learn to enjoy God and His ways. In many cases counselors are helping addicted people to lay aside their addictions, but counselors and recovery clinics are generally doing a poor job of helping addicts to enjoy God and the Christian life, yet it is only as believers learn to enjoy God that they will have the desires of their hearts met.

The reason for this is that many counselors and recovery professionals do not have adequate biblical training to disciple a recovering addict. But also, discipleship is a long, hard process compared to putting aside an addiction. It takes a significant amount of time and effort to help an addicted person reach the goal of godliness.

Paul says, "Discipline yourself for the purpose of godliness" (1 Tim. 4:7). The word *discipline* has to do with the idea of exercise—in this case, spiritual exercise. Someone has to oversee and help train the recovering addict as he or she goes through spiritual exercises: prayer, reading God's Word, fellowshiping with other believers, and sharing Christ with the lost. It is hard work, but it is worth it, and it is absolutely necessary to ensure that the addicted person will not have a relapse or simply move to a different addiction. This is where the need for long-term accountability and support come in.

Recovery organizations like Alcoholics Anonymous have long championed the concept of accountability and support. In these recovery movements the addict is given a "buddy" who is available for help and support day or night. The addict also has group meetings to attend which lend support and encouragement.

First Thessalonians 5:14 says, "Support the weak." The word *support* means to literally "hold one's self over against another."[6] The term *weak* refers to those believers who are particularly susceptible to fall into various sins, that is, addictions.[7] It is the responsibility of the local church not only to help Christians strip off addictions and to disciple them, but also to support those who are spiritually weak until they have learned to enjoy godliness. Discipleship and support is what is often missing in the local church and in Christian counseling. This is what is needed in order to effectively help those with addictions.

In the spring of 1993 I taught a seminary class on the subject of counseling. In my class was a Christian counselor working in association with a local church. The woman was a registered nurse as well as a trained counselor. She was a real asset to the class, and I learned many things from her during the course of the semester. One day she approached me after class and explained that she had been counseling with a couple of very addicted individuals and was making some progress, but not enough. Then she told me that she had begun to incorporate discipling as an integral part of her counseling process. She told me with great excitement that now she was really seeing the kind of progress she was hoping for. She finished her remarks by saying, "Discipleship was what I was missing, and it has made a tremendous difference!" Discipleship makes the difference in many situations between ministering to addicts and really helping them to break free.

Notes

[1]Markus Barth, "Ephesians 4–6," *The Anchor Bible,* Vol. 34A. Garden City, NJ: Doubleday, 1974. p. 505

[2]William Playfair, *The Useful Lie.* Wheaton, IL: Crossway, 1991, p. 55.

[3]Ibid., p. 23.

[4]See chapter 8.

[5]Fred Smith, *Learning To Lead.* West Orange, NJ: Leadership Library, 1986, p. 73.

[6]D. Edward Hiebert, *The Thessalonian Epistles.* Chicago: Moody Press, p. 236.

[7]Ibid.

14. Pressure and Fear

SOME time ago a man approached me seeking sympathy, advice, and counsel. He was clearly hurting so I agreed to listen and do what I could to help. Immediately he poured out his tragic story to me. His wife had recently divorced him, leaving him emotionally and financially devastated. His children were grown, but they still lived at home, causing him no end of grief. To make a terrible situation even worse, his job was both extremely stressful and quite possibly about to be phased out. He felt as if his whole world was crashing in on him and the weight was more than he could bear. He was not only depressed about the past, but very anxious about the future.

As I listened to this man explain his awful situation, I hurt for him and I told him so. But he desired a lot more from me than sympathy, as important as that was. He wanted wise counsel. He was seeking concrete help to deal with his enormous problems.

I could have told him that God is in control and that everything that happened to him was a part of God's wise and loving plan. And, of course, this would be true (Rom. 8:28). I also could have told him that God expected him not to just sit back and let things happen, but to take control of his life and do what was wise and morally correct, and that God would hold him accountable for what he decided to do. And this would also be biblically correct (2 Cor. 5:10).

But many Christians seem unable to understand and to reconcile these two truths. This is a major reason why many Christians today feel stressed out and anxious. Christians, like the man I counseled with, need help to come to grips with both God's sovereignty and people's personal responsibility. But in order to begin to do so, one has to properly define certain terms.

Christians often talk about being under stress or being stressed out. This is popular terminology. However, biblically and technically speaking what people are referring to is *pressure* and their reaction to that pressure. It is also important to note that many Christians, including many Christian counselors, appear to assume that pressure is almost always bad for us and not at all what God intends.

But 1 Thessalonians 3:1–3 tells a different story.

> When we thought we could endure it no longer, we thought it best to be left behind at Athens alone; and we sent Timothy, our brother and God's fellow worker in the gospel of Christ, to strengthen and encourage you as to your faith, so that no man may be disturbed by these afflictions; for you yourselves know that we have been destined for this.

The word *afflictions* in verse 3 literally refers to pressure, and more specifically, pressure that causes "distresses . . .

brought about by outward circumstances."[1] The Christians at Thessalonica were being pressured and persecuted (1 Thess. 2:14). Paul was concerned that this pressure would disturb the faith of these young Christians so he sent Timothy to them to strengthen and encourage them (3:2–3). Paul reminds the Thessalonian Christians that "we have been destined for this" (3:3). The word *destined* refers to that which happens by divine decree—in other words, by God's decision.[2] Paul is saying that at least in some situations, God decides to put Christians under tremendous pressure.

God's wise and loving plans for us include putting us under pressure so that we can develop "perseverance, character, and hope" (Rom. 5:3–4). Most importantly, God desires us to be "conformed to the image of His Son," which sometimes requires intense pressure.

Christians need to recognize that pressure is a part of God's unchangeable plan for us and it can be good. Thus, we must not allow it to disturb our faith and we should stop trying to avoid it at any cost. *Pressure is not always bad.* If we fail to understand this pressure, it can cause us to become anxious. But what does it mean to be anxious or to suffer from anxiety?

Philippians 4:6 says, "Be anxious for nothing, but in everything by prayer and supplication with thanksgiving let your requests be made known to God."

The word *anxious* does not rule out legitimate concerns, particularly for the welfare of others (Phil. 2:20). But when one is anxious, one is unduly concerned.[3] When a person becomes so concerned about a present situation or what the future holds that one is fearful, that is anxiety.

As the authors of *Worry-Free Living* express it, "It's an emotion that a person experiences in the face of a perceived threat or danger."[4] But why would a Christian be afraid in the first place?

One possible reason is that the person does not understand that God is in complete control, and that nothing is going to happen that is not a part of God's eternal plan (Eph. 1:1). If a Christian has not been taught that everything that happens is ultimately by divine design, and that there is no such thing as an accident for the believer, then that person will be afraid and will probably be afraid to face what they fear.

Another reason why a believer might be fearful is that one has not sufficiently understood the love of God. First John 4:16 says, "We have come to know and have believed the love which God has for us. God is love." John continues in verse 18 by saying that "there is no fear in love; but perfect love casts out fear."

God is love and His love is "perfect." When a person truly understands the love of God, fear is not going to be a major problem because one knows that God will ultimately do what is best for one. But when a Christian fails to grasp the greatness of God's love for one, he or she will often be fearful and may, again, be afraid to face what he or she fears.

So pressure can make a Christian fearful if one does not sufficiently understand either God's sovereign control over one's life or God's great love for one. But it is not enough for a Christian to understand just one of these truths, one must believe both of them.

Rabbi Kushner, in his book *Why Bad Things Happen To Good People,* concluded after the death of his son that God is love, but He is not all-powerful. He says, "God too is pained by death, more than even you and I are; but there's nothing much he can do about it."[5]

If one believes that God is love, but not all-powerful, one is going to be fearful as one goes through life because God is not really able to ensure what is best for one. On the other hand, if a person believes that God is totally in control, but doesn't really care about people personally, that individual is also going to be fearful because God may not be willing to act on his or her behalf. God can only be trusted if He is both completely loving and totally in control. Lack of belief in regard to either one of these two truths is going to cause considerable anxiety in Christians. An example of this is found in chapters 13 and 14 of the book of Numbers.

In this historic account the people of Israel have been delivered by God from bondage in Egypt and are on the threshold of entering the Promised Land. By God's command spies are sent out to check out the land that God had promised to give them (13:1–2). Unfortunately, when the spies return, they deliver a "good news, bad news" report. The land is indeed good, but the inhabitants, they say, "are too strong for us" (13:27–31). The result is that the people of Israel reject the minority report of Joshua and Caleb and are afraid to enter the land (14:1–4). Why? Because they either had doubts about the love or the power of God, or both. Joshua and Caleb attempted to address those doubts in Numbers 14:7–9:

> The land we passed through to spy out is an exceedingly good land. If the LORD is pleased with us, then He will bring us into this land, and give it to us—a land which flows with milk and honey. Only do not rebel against the LORD; and do not fear the people of the land, for they shall be our prey. Their protection has been removed from them, and the LORD is with us; do not fear them.

Joshua and Caleb remind the people that the land God wants to give them is "exceedingly good." Their implied message is that God really wants what is best for His people. He truly cares about His own.

At the same time, Joshua and Caleb address the issue of God's power and control. They state that "the protection has been removed" from the people of Canaan, and that "the LORD is with us." Their final word, therefore, to the people of Israel is "do not fear."

Unfortunately, the people of Israel did not believe that God was both loving and sovereign, so they were fearful and they rebelled against God. The consequences of this action were quite severe, but they brought it all on themselves because they refused to believe in spite of all the miracles that God had done on their behalf (14:11).

Gary Collins says that "beliefs have a great bearing on one's anxiety level. If God is seen as all-powerful, loving, good, and in ultimate control of the universe (which is biblical teaching), then there can be trust and security even in the midst of turmoil."[6]

This is not to say that every Christian who is anxious and fearful has no understanding of the truth or no faith at all. What needs to be clear is that this is a major reason for anxiety among Christians, and to the extent that a believer lacks faith in God in these particular areas, he or she is going to be correspondingly fearful.

My concern is that many Christian counselors do not seem to share Collins' conviction that theological "beliefs have a great bearing on one's anxiety level." If they do, there is little doubt that they are addressing this issue in an inadequate way.

If a Christian has never been told that God is both loving and sovereign, then in those cases insight from God's Word in a counseling setting could be sufficient to address this particular issue. However, if a Christian has been taught these truths, but doesn't fully believe them, then the issue probably has to be settled in a discipling relationship.

When a Christian has doubts about either God's love or sovereign control, almost certainly that believer is disappointed or disillusioned with God.[7] And this is a problem that requires discipling, not just counseling. The counselor will need to explore with the counselee what has led him or her to doubt God, and should attempt to address those concerns with counseling, particularly from Scripture. Nevertheless, the disappointed or disillusioned Christian will need to be in a discipling relationship where the love of God can be concretely seen in the life of the discipler and the discipler can demonstrate his or her belief in the sovereign control of God. Christians who are fearful due to insufficient faith need to not only hear the truth but see it demonstrated and lived out by fellow believers. Anything less will not be enough to help them with their fears.[8]

In addition to the major issue of proper belief and the need for discipleship, there is another matter that needs clarification and correction in regard to the problem of anxiety. Many Christian counselors believe that there is a difference between fear and anxiety.

For instance, the authors of *Worry-Free Living* state that

> many of us diagnose ourselves as being anxious when what we mean is that we feel fear. Often people use the words "anxiety" and "fear" interchangeably without realizing that a shade of difference exists between them. Uncertainty is a key element of anxiety, but not of fear. If you know what you are worried about, you're experiencing fear. If you're suffering from uneasiness and tension but you don't know why, that's anxiety. True anxiety is being afraid but having no idea what it is that you fear.

This alleged distinction between anxiety and fear may not seem like a problem worth mentioning, but in fact it is.

First of all, assuming for the moment that this distinction is valid, it still makes no difference in regard to how an anxious Christian should respond. Whether one is fearful about something one is certain about or anxious about something one is uncertain about does not matter. The problem is still a matter of faith. If God is loving and in control of all things, known and unknown, the believer's response should be to trust Him regardless. And no matter how one slices up anxiety, the basic emotion involved in "true anxiety is being afraid."[9]

Why is seeing anxiety apart from fear a problem in counseling? Besides the fact that it is an unnecessary distinction, it can also cause problems in determining exactly what the counselee is afraid of.

When a counselor views anxiety as an unknown fear, he or she often pursues what he or she thinks is the problem rather than what the counselee knows it is. The result is an erroneous diagnosis. When the error is finally discovered, the client can become very disillusioned, and the credibility of the counselor can be irrevocably damaged.

This is why I agree with Gary Collins when he says, "Never underestimate the counselee's insights into the reasons for his or her own anxiety."[10] One may not initially or fully understand why one thinks, feels, and acts the way one does. But with the help of the Spirit (1 Cor. 2:15–16), God's Word (Heb. 4:12–13), and a wise counselor who encourages the counselee to trust God and to honestly evaluate his or her heart and mind, the believer is truly capable of determining what one is afraid of and why one is fearful.

God's control, our responsibility

Let's turn again to the first issue of reconciling God's sovereign control with personal responsibility. Once the counselee has begun to accept, or to more fully embrace God's loving and sovereign control, the issue of personal responsibility needs to be addressed. But how does one know where one's personal responsibility begins and God's sovereignty ends? The answer is that whenever a particular matter is out of one's control, one must trust God and cast one's fears onto Him.

Years ago the Holmes and Rahe stress test was developed to help people evaluate how much stress they were experiencing. Life impacting situations like pregnancy, death of a close friend, and even vacation were assigned numerical values in order to give people some idea of where they are emotionally. The purpose for this test was undoubtedly to help people deal with their stress. But as Hawkins, Meier, and Minirth point out,

> Many of the events shown on the chart are out of
> our control. Christmas is going to come every Decem-
> ber 25 whether we're ready or not, the death of a spouse,
> the end of a school year, and restructured work hours of-
> ten occur without our consent or input. Like it or not,
> this might be the hand we're dealt. How we choose to
> play it is up to us.[11]

This is exactly the point. Whenever something is out of one's control, the individual has to decide how he or she is going to choose to play it. For the Christian the decision has to do, first of all, with whether or not one is going to trust in God's love and power. But just because one decides to trust God does not mean that the person will be totally fearless. In difficult circumstances it is impossible not to have some doubts with accompanying fears. However, it is one thing to have them, it is another to dwell on them (Phil. 4:8). Rather than listening to satanic lies about one's self (Rev. 12:10) or entertaining doubts about God, one must follow the instructions of 1 Peter 5:7, which says, "Cast all your anxiety on him because he cares for you" (NIV).

Most Christians know this verse and realize that they need to give their fears over to God. They know that they should simply tell God what they are afraid of and let Him handle it (Phil. 4:6). Nevertheless, many do not seem to recognize that this procedure has to be repeated as often as it is needed. In extremely difficult situations, Satan will try to undermine one's faith, and doubts will frequently cross our minds. Therefore, one may need to apply the procedure of 1 Peter 5:7 many, many times in the course of a day. This is not due to a lack of faith, but rather to the relentless assault of the powers of darkness (Eph. 6:12). There is no need to feel guilty about having to keep giving one's fears over to God.

This is not to deny, however, that there can be significant periods of inner peace even when one is under tremendous pressure. If one faithfully follows the instructions in Philippians 4:6–9, the promise is that "the peace of God, which surpasses all comprehension, shall guard your hearts and your minds in Christ Jesus" (Phil. 4:7). But even as God's peace stands guard over our hearts and minds, when satanic forces attack in the form of accusations and lies, there will be turmoil as the battle rages until the Christian refuses to listen anymore, casts his or her fears on God, and then goes on to positive thoughts and actions.

This, of course, is easier said than done. No question about it. And once again this is where discipleship is so crucial and why it is needed along with counseling. A Christian under pressure will be assaulted by many fears, and in some cases, may be able to fight them off alone. In other cases, weekly counseling sessions may be sufficient to keep the pressured believer from succumbing to fear. But in many cases, and with severe situations, one is going to need another believer to help bear the burden (Gal. 6:2) and to hold one up when one feels weak (1 Thess. 5:14). Someone will have to be available to encourage and pray for such a person perhaps on short notice and maybe in the middle of the night. Few counselors are willing or able to provide this kind of support and accountability, but this is often what is required to help pressured Christians who are struggling with situations out of their control. The question is, how does one know if a situation is truly out of one's control?

Our control, God's responsibility

When a Christian begins to feel pressure, and identifies its source, perhaps with the aid of a wise counselor, one then needs to determine whether this is pressure sovereignly allowed by God or something over which God expects one to exercise some control. The believer should not always assume that whatever is happening to him or her is completely God's will. Believers always have the responsibility to do what is right, but they also have the responsibility to do what they deem best.

When the apostle Paul explained that pressure is something that believers are destined for, he also reassured his readers that "we thought it best to be left behind and we sent Timothy . . . to strengthen and encourage you" (1 Thess. 3:1–2).

The term *best* can refer to that which is "well-pleasing" to either God or people.[12] Obviously, a Christian must decide what is pleasing to God first and foremost. But when it is not absolutely clear that God wants one under pressure, the believer should look long and hard at things that he or she can do to relieve the pressure.

For example, suppose one is found to have a cancerous growth. One should not necessarily conclude that God wants one to die and go on to glory. If there are treatment options that are not manipulative or sinful, he or she can pursue those until it is clear that God is ready to take him or her home. It is not easy or simple to determine God's will in these situations. That is why believers need wise counsel. Our actions are manipulative, and therefore wrongfully motivated if we are only concerned about what we want and not primarily about what will bring glory to God (1 Cor. 10:31). Our actions to relieve pressure are also sinful if they involve doing what we know is wrong. But when one believes one's motives to be largely right (they are never completely pure) and one's plan of action to be free of sin, then one must step out in faith realizing that a sovereign God can stop us with a mere word. And when it is perfectly clear that God wants us in a pressure situation we must trust Him and not fear.

According to 2 Corinthians 12:7–10, Paul was given a "thorn in the flesh" by God. He asked God three times to remove it but after the third entreaty, Paul believed that God gave him a definite and final "no." Therefore, Paul accepted this thorn and went on with what God wanted him to do in spite of it. Actually, according to Paul, it made him strong.

How do we know when to stop looking for ways to eliminate our pressure? When we have done everything we can do that is neither manipulative nor clearly sinful, and the pressure is still there, God wants it there and the believer must trust and obey without fear. And because of the difficulty of doing this, believers who are struggling to accept divinely ordained pressure without fear often need counseling and discipling.

I know a man who is under terrible pressure. His wife has threatened to leave him and he loves her dearly. He realizes that his behavior has alienated her and he is working hard to make up for the past and to win her affection back. Unfortunately, what has been done over years cannot be undone overnight. Therefore, he must also be patient and wait to see if what he hopes for will transpire. He is trusting in God, following God's Word, and listening carefully to counselors like myself. But there is no guarantee that she will remain with him, even if he does what is right. Furthermore, Satan is assaulting him with all sorts of accusations and lies, as well as regular reminders of what he has done to contribute to the demise of his marriage. He is being racked by guilt, doubts, and fears.

I meet with him as often as possible, but he is under incredible pressure every minute of the day. He needs more help than I can provide. Therefore, we enlisted the help of another man who is a mature Christian and friend. They meet together regularly for encouragement and prayer. But beyond even this, whenever the pressure seems to be too much and fears begin to overwhelm him, this struggling person can call this brother in Christ any time and he is available for comfort, prayer, even physical support if necessary. This is what Christians who are under intense pressure often need. Counseling is simply not enough.

Notes

[1]W. Bauer, W. F. Arndt, F. W. Gingrich, *Greek-English Lexicon*. Chicago, IL: U of Chicago Press, 1957, p. 362.
[2]Ibid., p. 502.
[3]Ibid., p. 506.
[4]Don Hawkins, Paul Meier, and Frank Minirth, *Worry-Free Living*. Nashville, TN: Thomas Nelson, 1989. p. 25.
[5]Harold Kushner, *Why Bad Things Happen To Good People*. Avenal, NJ: Outlet Book, 1986, p. 51.
[6]Gary Collins, *Christian Counseling*. Irving, TX: Word, 1991, p. 84.
[7]See Chapter 8 for a review of this concept.
[8]See Chapter 7 for a review of what is involved in discipling someone.
[9]Hawkins, Meier, and Minirth, p. 26.
[10]Gary Collins, p. 87.
[11]Hawkins, Meier, and Minirth, p. 40.
[12]W. Bauer, W. F. Arndt, F. W. Gingrich, p. 319.

15. Anger

CLIFF was as kind and mild-mannered a husband and father as you'd ever want to meet. He worked hard, made a decent living, was active in church, and loved to putter in his garden.

One summer day Cliff pulled his year-old lawn mower out of the shed and rolled it onto his beautifully landscaped back yard. He attached the bagger, set the controls on "START," and pulled the cord. Nothing. He pulled again. The engine turned over a couple of times, coughed, then died. He pulled again, again, and again. With each vigorous pull of the cord the engine belched smoke and gas fumes but wouldn't start.

Finally, after another hearty pull, the engine roared to life. Cliff straightened up and adjusted the throttle, but before he could take a step the engine died again. He stared at the mower and sighed deeply. Then he tried to restart it—once, twice, three times—but it wouldn't kick in. After glaring at the mower for several seconds, Cliff turned and walked toward the house.

Janice had noticed through the kitchen window that her husband was having trouble with the mower. "Is the mower broken?" she asked as Cliff walked in the back door and through the kitchen. He didn't answer her, didn't even acknowledge her presence. He just walked past her and down the hall to the den. In a couple of moments he came back through the kitchen carrying his prized deer-hunting rifle and a handful of shells. "Cliff?" Janice called to him in a tone of mild alarm. "Cliff, what are you doing?" Again Cliff walked past her and out the back door as if she were invisible. Janice held her breath as she watched him from the window.

Cliff walked to within ten feet of the lawn mower, then stopped. He methodically slid several shells into the rifle's magazine. Then he bolted a shell into the chamber, lifted the rifle, and took aim at the defenseless machine. Pow-clang! Pow-clang! Pow-clang! With each direct hit the lawn mower shuddered, and sparks and tiny shreds of metal exploded from it. It was a wonder that Cliff wasn't struck by the shrapnel.

After emptying the magazine into the lawn mower, Cliff calmly walked back into the house and retired to the den to clean his gun, closing the door behind him. Janice stood in the kitchen dumbfounded. She had never before seen such a change of character in her meek and mild husband. He was never one to display his emotions—until now! And it frightened her to wonder what other startling quirks might be lurking beneath Cliff's quiet, confident exterior.[1]

You may not struggle with anger to the same extent as this man, but anger is a problem for almost all of us at one time or another. There are several reasons why believers in Jesus Christ continue to struggle with anger even after getting extensive counseling to deal with it.

The first reason has to do with the fact that many tend to view anger, and emotions in general, in a negative way. These believers would probably not explicitly say that emotions are "bad," but they are, nevertheless, suspicious of emotions, concerned about being overly-emotional, and very reluctant to share their feelings with anyone.

A man recently stopped by my office unannounced. I did not know him but I could tell that he was very upset and nervous, so I asked him to come in. He told me that he had been driving around the church for forty-five minutes trying to get up the courage to speak with me. He then went on to explain that he was not only a Christian, but he was also involved in full-time Christian ministry and had been for years. Then came the bombshell. He said, "I have never really shared how I feel about anything with anybody." I was somewhat surprised and I asked him if he was also including his wife. He nodded affirmatively. At this point, for the first time in his life, he shared with another person how he really felt about a whole range of issues and events. It was extremely difficult for him, but he did it.

This man is not alone. There are many like him out there. Churches are full of them—people who deep down feel that feelings are not quite right and that they should not be acknowledged or expressed. But the Bible does not teach or endorse this position.

According to Genesis 1:27, both men and women are created in the image of God. Part of having that image means that we are emotional beings. God becomes angry in certain situations (Num. 14:11–12) and therefore, so do we. If God has emotions and expresses them, then having emotions and expressing them cannot be intrinsically wrong. In fact, God wants us to acknowledge our emotions and to express them properly, rather than deny or suppress them.

Ephesians 4:26 says, "Be angry, and yet do not sin . . . ." This verse contains two parts. The first is to "be angry," and the second is to "not sin" when angry. Our first responsibility is to acknowledge the anger when we are angry. As Neil

Anderson says, "You have no control over a primary emotion when it is triggered."[2] One cannot simply decide to become angry or not to become angry. But a person can suppress or deny an emotion, refusing to acknowledge how he or she is feeling. Thus God validates our anger as a legitimate emotion. We therefore do not need to suppress or deny it. Why is this so important? To answer this question one must first understand the God-ordained purpose for emotions.

Why emotions?

In the book of Jonah, we have the historical account of God's effort to draw a city away from sin and to Himself. God commissioned Jonah to go to Nineveh and call them to repentance. Jonah first refused, but God painfully persuaded him to fulfill his assignment and Jonah did. The result is that Nineveh repented and the city was spared God's awesome wrath. However, when Jonah realized that God was not going to destroy Nineveh, "he became angry" (4:1), and he asked that God take his life (4:3). God responded to his anger, not with condemnation or rebuke, but with a pointed question: "Do you have good reason to be angry?" (4:4).

The first purpose for emotions like anger is to help us recognize what we really believe and how we think. Emotions are the windows of our minds and souls. Jonah's anger alerted him to the fact that he did not truly appreciate God's love and mercy (4:2), then God went on to correct his faulty thinking by using a plant and a worm as an object lesson (4:6–11).

Emotion has been given to us by God so that we can bring our convictions and thoughts back in line with His truth. When we deny or suppress our emotions we short-circuit that God-ordained process. That is why God acknowledges our emotions such as anger. But with his acknowledgment, God also commands us not to sin (Eph. 4:26).

One reason for this command is obvious. Sin offends God and is wrong. But why the command do not sin in the context of acknowledging one's anger? The reason, once again, is directly related to God's divine purpose for emotions. Emotions not only help us to know what we truly believe and think, but they also motivate us to do what is right.

At first glance, James 1:20 appears to deny this. James says, "The anger of man does not achieve the righteousness of God." But we need to look more closely at this verse.

The word *anger* here refers to a "strong and persistent feeling of indignation," that is, bitterness or resentment, as opposed to another word in the New Testament which refers to an outburst or a fleeting experience of anger.[3] It is true that deep-seated, entrenched anger does not "achieve the righteousness of God." But short-term anger, like other emotions, can motivate us to do that which does honor God.

Some Christians I know who now actively oppose abortion were not doing so until recently. Why the change? They saw photos of unborn children that had been aborted and it made them angry. Because of that anger they are now trying to do what they can to save these children. This is where the command in Ephesians 4:26 enters in. It is right to be angry about the killing of children, and this anger should motivate us to action, but our actions must be God-honoring, not sinful. One cannot allow one's anger over abortion to be expressed in sinful ways, like killing doctors who perform abortions. God wants us to acknowledge our feelings and to properly express and act on them. But we must not sin.

In his book *Encouragement: The Key to Caring* written with Dan Allender, Larry Crabb relates the following story:

> Early in my counseling practice I succeeded, after much effort, to help a particularly depressed woman admit to feeling hostile when her husband staggered home

drunk in the wee hours of the morning. She arrived for the next session wearing a look of smug satisfaction. "I think I'm cured," she announced. "When my husband came home two nights ago at two-thirty smelling like a bar, I really got in touch with my anger. I was really steaming! So I waited till he crawled into bed, then I got up, went to my closet, and threw every shoe I own at him. He was too drunk to even move, so I got him good! And I felt a whole lot better."[4]

Crabb learned from that incident, but some Christian counselors still implicitly approve of sinful expressions of emotion. The excuse that "at least he's learning to express his emotions" is unacceptable. There is an important balance involved in dealing with one's emotions. God commands us to acknowledge them, but He also commands us to act upon them in a way that honors Him and furthers His purposes.

Crabb beautifully summarizes how a Christian should handle his emotions in three principles:

1. Fully experience your emotions; feel them.
2. Use your emotions; evaluate what they reveal about your beliefs and purposes.
3. Be free to express every emotion, but limit expression by the purposes of love.[5]

Until believers understand and practice these three biblical principles, they will continue to struggle with all their emotions, not just anger.

At this point I want to get more specific in regard to the second principle. We do need to examine our feelings to see what they reveal about our thoughts and beliefs. But what in particular should one be looking for? In order to answer this question we need to define anger.

Anger is basically the emotion of frustration. When we are angry, it is because someone or something has kept us from accomplishing a personal goal or having something we deeply desire.

The reason Jonah was angry when God spared Nineveh is because he had his heart set on seeing them destroyed. The Assyrians, who inhabited Nineveh, were bitter enemies of Israel. Jonah hated the Assyrians and that is undoubtedly one of the primary reasons why he tried to avoid going to Nineveh. He may also have been afraid, and with good reason. The Assyrians were among the cruelest people who ever lived. But after divine discipline, he was more afraid of God than of the Assyrians. Nevertheless, he still hated them. God used the object lesson of the plant and worm to help correct his thinking. Jonah needed to learn compassion. His desire to see the Assyrians destroyed was sinful because it did not reflect God's compassion for people (Jon. 4:10–11).

Sometimes when we are angry it is because we have desires and goals that are clearly wrong and they are being blocked, like Jonah's. When this is the case we need to ask God to teach us to be willing to be more like Him. But what about when our desires and goals are biblical or not inherently wrong? What about those times when what we desire is what we need and those desires and goals are still frustrated?

There are a lot of angry people around, but probably none angrier than one man I know. He doesn't appear to be angry. He appears to be a healthy, intelligent, well-adjusted, and even cheerful person. But underneath is a volcano of anger just waiting to explode—and it does—all over his wife and family on frequent occasions. When I counseled with him, he acknowledged that he was angry. He was angry because no matter what he does he cannot achieve financial success. He worked hard for years, invested carefully and faithfully, giving a tenth of all his earnings to the Lord's work.

But in spite of all this, he feels that he has not arrived financially, and it really upsets him. Why?

One reason is that he wanted to be able to provide for his family in the future. His desire was to have enough money to guarantee that he would be able to take care of them no matter what happened. But the second reason has to do with his legitimate human need for significance. He felt that the only thing standing in the way of his feeling significant was his lack of business success. If that problem could be resolved or turned around, then his family would be financially secure and he would feel significant as a man and as a person. Until then, he said that he would be angry, and he felt that he had a right to be. How could one not be angry in his situation, he asked? Is there an answer?

First of all, it is not wrong to have our legitimate human needs met. And it is biblical to provide for one's own family (1 Tim. 5:8). But this man's beliefs need to be reassessed.

Philippians 4:19 states that "my God shall supply all your needs according to His riches in glory in Christ Jesus."

This is a promise from God to generously meet all the needs that a Christian has. I believe that this promise includes our emotional needs as well as our physical ones. But notice that God does not promise to meet our needs in the way we may desire or in accordance with our personal goals regarding the timing.

There is still plenty of time for God to make this man a financial success if that is what is needed for him to provide for his family. God's timing is always perfect. It may not seem that way at any given moment, but He not only knows what is best for us, but He acts on our behalf at exactly the right time.

Leslie Flynn, in his book *The Sustaining Power of Hope,* relates a moving story that beautifully illustrates the perfection of God's timing.

Toward the end of World War II a young sailor, fresh from the Pacific conflict and with limited furlough time, rejoiced when he was allotted a seat on a military C–46 out of Alameda Airport headed for Chicago where his girlfriend lived. Gliding through the gateway into the 21-seat plane, he buckled his safety belt and relaxed. The right propeller churned the air, then the left. The chocks were pulled from under the wheels. The plane was about to taxi for the takeoff. Suddenly outside was the stationmaster, wildly waving his arms. Behind him a vice-admiral waddled under the weight of two large duffel bags. "Hold that flight," hollered the stationmaster.

The sailor's heart sank. When the door opened, he heard three names, one of which was his. The three were told to get off the plane while the vice-admiral and his two bags took the three seats. Sitting dejectedly on the ground as the plane took off, the sailor looked up, "God, why did You let this happen to me? You know I want to get home!"

Happily, three hours later the sailor caught another plane for Chicago. That evening as the plane descended toward the Kansas City airport for a brief stop, huge searchlights flared all around. "Turn out those lights," shouted the pilot over his radio system. "We don't need them to land."

"Identify yourself," replied the tower. "Which flight are you?" The pilot identified his plane.

"Where's the flight that left Alameda three hours before you? It hasn't come in yet?"

The flight never did come in. Its wreckage was found in the Rockies some days later. Today, that sailor is a well-known radio announcer, Bob Murfin, who emcees the morning commuter-hour program over Chicago's Moody radio station, WMBI.[6]

This is one reason why James says, "Let everyone be ... slow to anger" (James 1:19). Christians need to believe that God is in control of all things and that He will meet our needs in His perfect time.

Now someone might wonder, "What if it's clear that God is not going to intervene or meet my need this side of glory?" In 2 Corinthians 12:7 Paul says that

> to keep me from exalting myself, there was given me a thorn in the flesh, a messenger of Satan to buffet me— to keep me from exalting myself. Concerning this I entreated the Lord three times that it might depart from me. And He said to me, "My grace is sufficient for you for my power is perfected in weakness . . . ."

There is much that we do not know about this "thorn in the flesh." But we do know that this "thorn" was from God, and that Paul did not think, initially, that he needed it. He asked God three times to take it away. It was undoubtedly a source of tremendous pain and frustration for him. However, God made it clear to him that he did need it to keep him from becoming proud and for God's power to be displayed in his weakness.

The point is that we do not always know what we need and we do not always understand how God works to glorify Himself in our lives. But God knows what we need and He is going to meet those needs even as He is bringing glory to Himself through our lives.

Rather than being angry or bitter with God, Paul said, "I am well content with weaknesses, with insults, with distresses, with persecutions, with difficulties, for Christ's sake, for when I am weak, then I am strong."

Why did Paul feel content rather than angry? Because his weakness made him strong. His legitimate human needs for love, acceptance, and significance were being met by God in spite of, and, perhaps, because of, his "thorn in the flesh."

Paul felt God's love and acceptance in a profound way and prayed that other Christians would come to understand "the love of Christ which surpasses knowledge" (Eph. 3:19). Paul also felt that he was a significant person in God's sight and that he had accomplished significant things with God's help (2 Cor. 12:11–12). Even though he had a terribly aggravating problem, Paul was content, not angry, because his most important needs were being met by God. And this can be true for us today if we simply recognize what God has already done for us and trust Him for tomorrow.

There are a lot of angry Christians and many of them are angry with God, although they may be reluctant to admit it. Listen to the confession of one such Christian.

> I will now tell you my most terrible secret. I get
> very mad at God sometimes, especially when he lets
> me get hurt. In fact, I will let a million cats out of
> the bag. I will tell all the doubters and unbelievers
> who are reading this a terrible secret most Christians
> do not tell: I think almost every believing Christian
> and probably almost every believing Jew and Mos-
> lem too, gets mad at God sometimes. This is a pretty
> well-kept secret, especially among evangelicals and
> fundamentalists.[7]

Christian anger with God is a much bigger and widespread problem than we want to admit. But if we believe that God is in control of all things (Eph. 1:11), then whatever happens to us is ultimately His will. So if we are angry, we are angry with God whether we admit it or not.

Jeremiah became angry with God when he was persecuted for proclaiming God's prophetic word to the people of

Judah, but he would not admit it. Instead, he said he was angry that he had been born and he expressed his hatred for life (Jer. 20:14–18). But as Lewis Smedes insightfully says, "Hating God's most precious gift is a believer's sneaky way to hate God."[8] Those who hate life or express anger over their lot in life are angry with the God who has either caused or allowed it.

Occasional or temporary anger may not be directed at God, but when we continue to be angry it indicates that we are not happy with the way God is running the universe, especially our part of it. Until one is willing to admit this, one cannot truly begin the healing process. When we have admitted our anger with God, the process has begun but it is far from over. The angry Christian must believe that God has promised to meet his or her needs and to do what is ultimately best for him or her (Rom. 8:28). Obviously, this involves trust. But how does a person trust someone that one feels has failed one terribly?

The answer is that he or she must get to know God a lot better. This is not going to happen overnight. It will require time and much effort. The Christian has to become reacquainted, as it were, with God through the study of Scripture and seeing God in the lives of fellow Christians. This is where discipling comes in once again. Counseling will often help, but in these situations it is not enough.

Notes

[1]David Stoop and Stephen Arterburn, *The Angry Man.* Irving, TX: Word, 1991, p. 11–12.

[2]Neil Anderson, *Victory Over the Darkness.* Ventura, CA: Regal, 1990, p. 196.

[3]D. Edmond Hiebert, *The Epistle of James.* Chicago: Moody Press, 1979, p. 126.

[4]Larry Crabb and Dan Allender, *Encouragement: The Key to Caring.* Winona Lake, IN: BMH Books, 1986, p. 64.
[5]Larry Crabb, *Understanding People.* Grand Rapids, MI: Zondervan, 1987, p. 188.
[6]Leslie Flynn, *The Sustaining Power of Hope.* Wheaton, IL: Victor, 1985, p. 65–66.
[7]Lewis Smedes, *Forgive & Forget.* San Francisco: Harper, 1984, p. 115.
[8]Ibid.

16. Forgiveness

It was very late at night when I got a phone call no pastor likes to receive. A man in our church, a deputy sheriff, had been struck by a car and was in the hospital. His wife, who called me, was obviously upset, but she was also relieved that he was alive and doing as well as he could. She very calmly explained to me what had happened.

Her husband had been manning a road block knowing that a criminal was loose in the area. When the thief approached the road block in his car, he realized he was about to be arrested and tried to crash past to escape. In doing so, he hit the officer with his car and injured him severely. But because of God's protection, he survived.

Shortly after this incident, the criminal was apprehended, convicted, and sent to prison. When the injured deputy, Bill Kreamalmyer, got out of the hospital, the Holy Spirit began to encourage him not only to forgive this man but to go visit him in prison. The purpose was to tell him he had forgiven him for Christ's sake. Bill did not know what kind of reception he would meet, but to his surprise, the offender was very open. When Bill informed him that he had forgiven him and why, the prisoner cried and expressed his desire to receive God's forgiveness through Jesus Christ. Bill had the opportunity to lead this man to the Lord because he was willing to forgive.

We are frequently confronted with the need to forgive and to be forgiven, because Christians are not immune to being hurt or to hurting others in this fallen world. Having someone physically injure one by running one down is painful and hard to forgive, but many of us have been hurt just as surely and severely by the words and attitudes of others. Physical and emotional wounds are equally painful. The pain can seem unbearable and the offender unforgivable. But forgiveness is critical for the offender and the offended.

Many Christians realize that forgiveness is the right thing to do. But they still struggle with forgiveness. Why is this the case? Many believers are genuinely confused about what forgiveness is. A lot of Christians think that they have forgiven someone who hurt them, but they continue to struggle with anger, distrust, recurring memories, and deep pain. This causes us to wonder if we really have forgiven. So what is forgiveness all about?

Forgiveness is a conscious decision not to hold something against someone who has hurt or offended us. This means it is also a decision to no longer be angry with that person. Neil Anderson says, "Forgiveness means resolving to live with the consequences of another person's sin."[1] Forgiveness does not mean that we no longer feel hurt when we remember what was done to us. In fact, we may feel great pain when we see the forgiven person or think about what that individual did. We may continue to experience emotional pain until we actually see God using it for good in our lives. Just because you still hurt does not mean you have not forgiven.

But if you still feel angry when you remember the offense or see the person who sinned against you, you have not forgiven the individual.

In his book, *The Secret of Loving*, Josh McDowell gives a personal example of what forgiveness is *not*.

> My eldest brother, Wilmot, was my parents' favorite, yet when he left the farm he sued them for 50 percent of everything they owned. For years I resented him for hurting my mother so badly and for the humiliating public display he made of our family problems.
>
> Not long after I became a Christian, God began to convict me of my bitterness toward Wilmot. So I wrote him a letter—the perfect model of how not to forgive someone. It was five pages long. The first four and nine-tenths pages listed everything he had done wrong and for which he needed forgiveness. I even added the charming statement, "You killed Mom," because I knew he had. Between my father's drunken abuse and Wilmot's lawsuit, my mother had just given up the will to live.
>
> At the close of the last page I wrote, "I have come to know Jesus Christ personally and I want you to know I forgive you." I signed it and then tacked on this P.S.: "I never want to see you again."[2]

Forgiveness means no longer holding something against another even though we may still feel hurt when we see the individual or think about what the person did to us. This being the case, forgiveness does not necessarily mean forgetting.

In Hebrews 8:12, the writer of Hebrews quotes God's words from Jeremiah 31:34, "I will be merciful to their iniquities, and I will remember their sins no more."

God is not saying here that He literally forgets sin. Rather the word *remember* indicates that even though God is aware of our sin, He is not going to punish us for it.[3] In a similar way, we cannot help but remember at times what someone has done to us. Nevertheless, if we choose to forgive, even as we recall painful events, the anger is gone. David Augsburger puts it this way,

> [Forgiving is] not a case of holy amnesia which erases the past. No, instead it is the experience of healing which draws the poison from the wound. You may recall the hurt, but you will not relive it! No constant reviewing, no rehashing of the old hurt, no going back to sit on the old gravestones where past grievances lie buried. True, the hornet of memory may fly again, but forgiveness has drawn its sting. The curse is gone. The memory is powerless to arouse or anger.[4]

So just because you still remember and still hurt because you remember, these feelings do not mean you have not forgiven. The issue is anger. If you are still angry with that person, you have not completely forgiven him or her.

Possibly at this point you realize that you are not angry at a person who sinned against you but you are concerned because you still do not trust that person. Does this lack of trust also mean that you have not forgiven? My response to this question comes from Luke 15:11–32.

The story of the Prodigal Son tells how he insisted on his share of his father's estate (15:12) and then went out and spent it foolishly on "loose living" (15:13). After he was destitute and reduced to feeding swine, he came to his senses and decided to return home (15:14–19). His father saw him coming "while he was still a long way off" and ran out to welcome him home with open arms. The father then dressed up the wayward son and prepared a feast to celebrate his homecoming (15:20–24). The older son, when he found out what was happening, was angry, and he approached his father with great indignation about the situation (15:25–30). But the father's reply is very instructive. He said, "My child, you have always been with me, and all that I have is yours. But we had to be merry and rejoice, for this brother of yours was dead and has begun to live, and was lost and has been found" (15:31–32).

The older son clearly had not forgiven his younger brother and he was probably even concerned that his father was going to redistribute what was left of his estate. Even though the father had definitely forgiven his youngest son he made it quite clear that the remainder of his estate belonged to the older son (15:31). This was only fair, but I also believe that the father was making a statement about his level of trust in his younger son. He had forgiven him, but there was no way he would trust the Prodigal Son with any more money.

Forgiveness also does not mean that you must tolerate sin. A young wife and mother told me of her decision to forgive her mother for continually manipulating her for attention. But she tearfully continued, "What am I supposed to do when I see her next week? She is no different. She will undoubtedly try to come between me and my family as she always does. Am I supposed to let her keep ruining my life?"

No, forgiving someone doesn't mean that you must be a doormat to their continual sin. I encouraged her to confront her mother lovingly but firmly, and tell her that she would no longer tolerate destructive manipulation. It's okay to forgive another's past sins and, at the same time, take a stand against future sins.[5]

Just because we have forgiven someone does not mean that we should be naive or foolish in our future dealings with the person. We should not put ourselves in a position to be hurt again. Forgiveness means that I will not hold the past against someone, but trust means that the person has to show me that he is not going to hurt me again. We must forgive, but we do not have to trust, although we should be open to letting the offender earn our trust again.

Now there is yet another popular misunderstanding about forgiveness. Some Christians think that if one's offer to forgive is not accepted by the offender, then forgiveness is somehow thwarted.

It is true that one of the purposes of forgiveness is reconciliation. And if someone refuses to accept our forgiveness, reconciliation cannot take place. However, true forgiveness can occur even if the person being forgiven refuses to accept our forgiveness, and even if the person being forgiven does not know that we have forgiven him or her.

When Jesus was on the cross, people were executing Him, dividing His clothes, mocking Him, and sneering at Him, but He said, "Father, forgive them, for they do not know what they are doing" (Luke 23:34). Few, if any, of these people accepted His forgiveness, if they even heard Christ utter His words of forgiveness. Nevertheless, Christ was legitimately forgiving all those who took part in His execution, including you and me, because it was our sins, as well, that caused Him to be nailed to that cruel cross.

We can legitimately forgive people even if they don't know it or accept it. When we do, we are right before God and forgiveness has positive effects in our lives. But it is true that forgiveness has to be received by others for it to have its beneficial effects in their lives. And going back to Christ's offer of forgiveness, we have to personally accept it in order to obtain eternal life and its benefits (Acts 10:43).

The question some may ask is, "Why should I forgive?" I have no doubt that many reading this chapter have been wronged in the most despicable and terrible of ways. I am sure that almost every person alive has been hurt or offended in a way that, humanly speaking, is beyond forgiveness. Nevertheless, I have to maintain that forgiveness is the best thing for you to do. Why? Because Christ commanded it.

In Matthew 18:21, Peter asked Jesus, "Lord, how often shall my brother sin against me and I shall forgive him. Up to seven times?" Peter thought that he was being very generous because the rabbis of his day said that three times was enough.[6] However, Christ replied, "Up to seventy times seven" (18:22), which should be translated "seventy-seven times." This was a popular Jewish expression referring to essentially an unlimited number of times. It is like a person today saying "a million times." Thus, Christ was saying that we should forgive people without limit. However, I realize that this simply raises the question again of "why?"

Jesus, anticipating the question, told the story of a king who had servants who owed him money (18:23–35). One servant in particular owed him an incredible amount of money, over ten thousand talents. This was more than the servant could repay in a hundred lifetimes. At first the king was going to sell him and his family for whatever he could get. But when the servant begged for more time, the king felt compassion for him and forgave him the entire debit. Unfortunately, the slave did not learn from this wonderful experience, but instead went out and found a fellow slave who owed him money and had him put in prison until he paid what he owed. When word of this got back to the king, he was understandably furious. He called the ungrateful servant back and handed him over for punishment until his debt was paid. Christ ends the parable with these words, "So shall my heavenly Father also do to you, if each of you does not forgive his brother from your heart" (18:35).

Is Christ saying that our forgiveness of others is the condition of God's forgiveness? I think not. That understanding of this passage and Matthew 6:14–15 runs contrary to the tenor of the entire New Testament. Ephesians 2:8–9, Titus 3:5, and John 6:28–29 are abundantly clear that we are not in any way saved by our works. We are forgiven by God and saved on the basis of faith in Christ.

Christ is pointing out here that because we have been so wonderfully and undeservedly forgiven, we ought to forgive others an unlimited number of times. And our willingness to do so indicates whether or not we understand how much we have been forgiven.

Goldie Bristol's daughter, Diane, was brutally murdered a number of years ago. She and her husband are Christians and they made a very public decision to forgive their daughter's murderer. Many people were appalled—even many Christians. When Goldie was questioned about her decision on one occasion, she said this:

> When I stop to realize how much Christ had to forgive—my terrible debt of sin against Him, one I could never have paid, nor did I deserve to have it paid, yet God, in His unspeakable love for me absorbed my debt in its entirety—how can I not forgive? How dare I withhold forgiveness. Only those of us who have never needed forgiveness dare entertain the thought, *I won't forgive.* And who of us has not needed forgiveness?[7]

Goldie was right. When we realize how much we have been forgiven for Christ's sake, we have no grounds for saying, "No, I won't forgive." We should forgive because God commands us to do so, but also because we have been forgiven for everything we have ever done or ever will do.

What forgiveness does for us

But, as if this isn't enough, we should also forgive because withholding forgiveness is dangerous and harmful for us. Take the following story, for instance.

A couple in Kentucky had an only child who was killed at the age of eighteen by a drunk driver in a car accident one mile from their home. The couple was outraged and "dedicated their lives to punishing the drunken driver who had killed their only child." Motivated by hatred, they observed his every court appearance and followed him to the county jail to ensure that he was actually serving his time. The court process was slow and did not punish the driver as severely as the mother wanted. "Every time it would be delayed, I would get more upset and my hatred for him would grow," the mother recalled to a reporter. After two years of this, the couple realized that their anger toward the driver was beginning to consume them and their efforts at revenge were only hurting themselves, so they decided to forgive him and help him rebuild his life. "The hate and bitterness I was feeling were destroying me. . . . I needed to forgive Tommy to save myself."[8]

Withholding forgiveness, which fosters hate and bitterness, is like a cancer. It eats away at one spiritually and emotionally until one's life is ruined. Forgiveness is not only right, it is always the best thing we can do for ourselves. You may think that your life is as bad as it can be because of what someone has done to you. But it can get worse, if you refuse to forgive.

Revenge sometimes looks very attractive. But once again, appearances can be deceiving. The fact is that you can rarely cause the person who hurt you as much pain as he or she has caused you. This is one reason God says, "Never take your own revenge, beloved, but leave room for the wrath of God, for it is written, 'Vengeance is Mine, I will repay,' says the Lord" (Rom. 12:19). And He goes on to say, "Do not be overcome by evil, but *overcome evil with good*" (12:21). This is what brings true healing. Listen to a woman who knows.[9]

Dear Abby,

I have read many letters in your column from people who say they cannot forgive. What they really mean is, they will not forgive. Abby, withholding forgiveness hurts only you. It can eat you alive.

I want to tell you what I was able to forgive in hopes that it will help people who are harboring petty grudges to forgive, and get on with their lives.

Lee and I have been married for 10 years. Last year he became completely burned out at his job and also suffered a severe back injury. I was expecting our fourth baby and we have another family sharing our home. All this created a very explosive atmosphere, and Lee flipped out. Our baby was born and developed mononucleosis at three weeks. Lee announced that he didn't love me anymore, and he left me.

The other family moved out suddenly, and I was alone with a sick newborn and three other small children. I couldn't eat or sleep. I lost 47 pounds, got hooked on tranquilizers and had a nervous breakdown. Lee came back, put me in a mental hospital, then proceeded to have an affair with my best friend of 20 years (the affair lasted four months).

While I was in the hospital, my best friend's husband broke into our house and caught his wife and Lee in bed together. He told Lee that he could have her—then Lee and my girlfriend became "engaged." They told me later that they had planned to drive me to commit suicide so I would be out of the way.

After I was released from the hospital, Lee tricked me into a false reconciliation. Two hours after making love to me, he stood me up at the airport and took his girlfriend to Florida. Meanwhile, my kids were aware of everything that was going on, and my 7-year-old kept begging me to shoot him in the head because he didn't want to live. It was terrible. We lost our home, so the children and I moved into my parents' attic with no heat—during a Pennsylvania storm.

Suddenly, Lee came to his senses and broke up with his girlfriend. Her husband forgave her and she went back to him and their three children. And guess what? I forgave Lee and took him back. I got counseling, went to church and kept reading my Bible. I'm off the pills, eating normally, and our family is intact. We got our house back, Lee is totally repentant, and we have restructured our lives to avoid anything that could be destructive to our family.

Two weeks ago, I went to my girlfriend and told her I forgave her. We cried together and talked for six hours. Forgiveness, when it is least deserved, has true healing powers. In forgiving her, I released her of all guilt, and now God is able to work in my life.

I still feel a little insecure at times, but I'm much better today than I was six months ago. A life filled with thoughts of revenge and bitterness is no life at all. Abby, if you think this letter will help others to forgive, you have my permission to print it with my name.

Donna Stewart
Hilltown, PA

I hope you are convinced that forgiveness is right and best for you. But you may still have some questions about how to go about forgiving someone. Neil Anderson offers these steps to follow in forgiving another.

Here are 12 simple steps you can use to walk through the process of forgiving someone who hurt you in the past. Following these steps will help you unchain yourself from the past and get on with your life:

1.   Write on a sheet of paper the names of the persons who offended you. Describe in writing the specific wrongs you suffered (e.g., rejection, deprivation of love, injustice, unfairness, physical, sexual or emotional abuse, betrayal, neglect, etc.)

2.   Face the hurt and the hate. Write down how you feel about these people and their offenses.

3.   Acknowledge the significance of the cross. It is the cross of Christ that makes forgiveness legally and morally right.

4.   Decide that you will bear the burden of each person's sin. (Gal. 6:1–2).

5.   Decide to forgive.

6.   Take your list to God and pray the following: "I forgive (name) and (list for offense)."

7.   Destroy the list.

8.   Do not expect that your decision to forgive will result in major changes in the other persons.

9.   Try to understand the people you have forgiven. They are victims also.

10.   Expect positive results of forgiveness in you.

11.   Thank God for the lessons you have learned and the maturity you have gained as a result of the offenses and your decision to forgive the offenders (Rom. 8:28–29).

12.   Be sure to accept your part of the blame for the offenses you suffered.[10]

At this point it is important to point out that forgiveness is not usually a one-time event but a process. You may make an initial decision to forgive, but that does not mean that you have completely or permanently forgiven. You must continue to work on forgiving and make the decision to forgive again if your anger and hate return. In some situations, complete and permanent forgiveness comes only after years of intense effort.

C. S. Lewis, Christian scholar and writer, struggled for many years to forgive a childhood teacher who made life miserable for him. Just before his death he wrote this letter to a friend.[11]

> Dear Mary,
> Do you know, only a few weeks ago I realized suddenly that I had at last forgiven the cruel schoolmaster who so darkened my childhood. I'd been trying to do it for years; and like you, each time I thought I'd done it, I found, after a week or so it all had to be attempted over again. But this time I feel sure it is the real thing . . . .
>
> Yours,
> Jack

Forgiveness is sometimes instantaneous. But often it is a process that takes a while. We should not be discouraged by this, but rather accept it and continue to work at forgiveness because even though the process is sometimes slow, it's worth it. However, the process should not involve forgiving God.

Forgiving God?

There are Christian counselors who encourage believers to forgive God when they perceive that God has treated them unfairly, or even wrongly. The first problem with this is that the Bible nowhere encourages us to forgive God. But the biggest problem with this procedure is that in the long term is sabotages the person's prospects for wholeness.

Forgiving God for a perceived wrong may help a person feel better about God in the short-term, but it also reinforces two errors that hinder long-term emotional and spiritual wellness.

First, if God sometimes needs to be forgiven, it implies logically, if not explicitly, that He has either sinned or made a mistake. But the Bible is quite clear that God is both righteous (John 17:25) and wise (Rom. 16:27). He neither sins nor makes mistakes. In order for us to move closer to wholeness in this life we need to realize that God only does what is right and best for us. Forgiving God is a practical denial of this truth, and a step in the wrong direction.

Second, if God sometimes needs to be forgiven, it implies that either He owes us something that He hasn't delivered or that we deserve better than what He has done. Both of these implications are false. God does not owe us anything. He has graciously provided salvation for us through Jesus Christ (Eph. 2:8), and He does many things for us because He is a good and gracious God. But He doesn't owe us anything. In order for us to move closer to wholeness in this life we need to realize that everything God does for us is grace. Until we realize this we will continue to be offended and hurt when God doesn't do what we think He should. And our relationship to Him will continue to be strained, or at the very least, not as close as we need it to be in order to experience eternal life here and now.

Rather than forgive God when we blame or accuse Him, we need to eventually go to Him as Job did and say:

> I know that Thou canst do all things, and that no purpose of Thine can be thwarted. Who is this that hides counsel without knowledge? Therefore I have declared that which I did not understand, things too wonderful for me, which I did not know. Hear, now, and I will speak; I will ask Thee, and do Thou instruct me. I have heard of Thee by the hearing of the ear; but now my eye sees Thee; Therefore, I retract, and I repent in dust and ashes. (42:2–6)

In order to forgive, we often need to understand what forgiveness is, why it should be done, and that it is often a process, not a single event. But make no mistake about it, forgiveness is worth it no matter what the cost or effort. As Billy Graham has often said, the three most healing words are "I forgive you." We all need to hear them and to say them.

Notes

[1]Neil Anderson, *Victory Over the Darkness.* Ventura, CA: Regal, 1990, p. 202.

[2]Josh McDowell, *The Secret of Loving.* Wheaton, IL: Tyndale, 1986, p. 78.

[3]W. Baur, W. F. Arndt, F. W. Gingrich, *Greek-English Lexicon.* Chicago: U of Chicago Press, 1957, p. 524.

[4]David Augsburger, *The Freedom of Forgiveness.* Chicago: Moody Press, 1977, p. 39.

[5]Neil Anderson, p. 202.

[6]D. A. Carson, *Expositor's Bible Commentary.* Grand Rapids: Zondervan, p. 405.

[7]Goldie Bristol and Carol McGinnis, *When It's Hard To Forgive.* Wheaton, IL: Victor, 1982, p. 60.

[8]Donald Sloat, *Dangers of Growing Up in Christian Home.* Nashville, TN: Thomas Nelson, p. 157–58.

[9]Dear Abby column.

[10]Neil Anderson, p. 203–205.

[11]Lewis Smedes, *Forgive & Forget.* New York: Pocket Books, 1984, p. 127.

17. Self-Esteem

In his book, *His Image . . . My Image,* Josh McDowell quotes an attractive woman who said this about herself.

> A worm doesn't adequately describe how I feel
> about myself. A worm can crawl underground and hide;
> he doesn't leave a trail behind him. I'm more like the
> ugly, slimy slugs on my patio. Everywhere they go they
> leave this horrible trail behind them. I'm like them; I
> mess up everything wherever I go.[1]

Can Christians really feel this way about themselves? The answer, unfortunately, is yes! As a matter of fact, many Christians do feel this way about themselves. Neil Anderson has said,

> Several years ago I conducted a little personal re-
> search to discover how many Christians are still victims
> of their flesh. I asked the same question to 50 consecu-
> tive Christians who came to see me to talk about prob-

lems in their lives: "How many of the following
characteristics describe your life: inferiority, insecurity,
inadequacy, guilt, worry, and doubt?" Everyone one of
the 50 answered, "All six."[2]

Perhaps you too have strong feelings of worthlessness
or inferiority. Clearly you are not alone. But maybe you are
not even sure that God wants you to feel better about yourself.
I believe He does! Each of us has a divinely created need for
security and significance and in Christ we can have these
needs met. But the question some have is, "If God wants us to
feel secure and significant, why then doesn't the Bible explicitly say so and directly address these needs? This is a legitimate question and it deserves a serious response.

It is true that the Bible does not explicitly state that we
each have a divinely created need for security and significance. It is also true that the Scripture does not directly
address these needs. But there are still clear indictors that God
wants us to feel secure and significant, and He has taken definite steps to meet those needs.

First John 3:1 says, "See how great a love the Father has
bestowed upon us, that we should be called children of God,
and such we are."

The Bible says that God has loved us in an astonishing
way. In Christ we are the "beloved" (1 John 3:2). God has
loved us because it is His nature to love (4:8), but it also follows that we *need* His love. Would God give us anything
superfluous that we do not need—that is not in our best interest? I think not. God loves us because He is love and because
everyone needs love.

Having established that, it is important to recognize that
love is the primary foundation for emotional security. When
one is loved, then one is emotionally secure. As 1 John 4:18
says, "There is no fear in love but perfect love casts out fear."

When we deeply understand God's perfect love for us, we will be secure, not afraid, and that is exactly what God wants for us. That is why He assures us of His love so many times in His Word. There is a common misunderstanding, however, about God's love in regard to our security and significance.

Some Christians believe that Christ's sacrifice on the cross indicates that we have intrinsic worth. As one person has put it, "You are 'worth Jesus' to God because that is what He paid for you. That is His statement of your value."[3] Don Matzat points out the fallacy of this line of thinking.

> A recent television newscast reported the arraignment of a serial killer who has admitted responsibility for at least fifteen murders. The judge set his bail at $5 million! Would we use the same sort of reasoning to conclude that this man should feel good about himself and regard himself as an especially valuable human being, since the judge set his bail so high?[4]

It is true that we are "worth Jesus" to God, but not because of any intrinsic value that is in us. We were helpless and undeserving sinners God graciously loved anyway (Rom. 5:6–8), and because He loved us we now have tremendous value. We are now the "beloved." But not only this, we are "children of God" (1 John 3:1).

The fact that He calls us "children of God" is very important. It indicates that God wants us to realize that we are significant! It is true that He wants us to act like His children and like His son, Jesus Christ (Eph. 5:1–2). However, if that was all He wanted to accomplish, He could simply say, "Act like a child of mine should," and stop there. But in addition He tells us that we are "saints" (Eph. 1:1), "heirs of God and fellow heirs with Christ" (Rom. 8:17), "sons" of God (Gal. 4:5–6) and citizens of heaven (Phil. 3:20).[5] Clearly,

God wants us to know we are significant in Christ. Not because of any intrinsic importance in us, but because He has deemed us important. Why would He tell us we are "children of God" unless we have a built-in need for significance? Why would He risk giving us a big head unless we need to know that we are valuable in Christ? Now the question remains, Why doesn't God's Word encourage us to pursue these needs?

The answer is that God does not want us to pursue these needs. He wants us to pursue Him. He does address our need for security and significance, but indirectly. Self-esteem is a natural by-product of knowing who we are in Christ, and more importantly, knowing God well.

In Revelation 3:20, God says to the Laodicean church and to us, "Behold, I stand at the door and knock; if anyone hears My voice and opens the door, I will come in to him, and will dine with him, and he with Me."

Many people quote this verse in evangelistic efforts, and perhaps this is a legitimate application. However, this verse primarily has to do with fellowship. God is saying here that He wants to spend time with us. In the ancient Middle East, as in many cultures today, meals served a purpose beyond the consumption of food. Meals were a time to enjoy other people and grow closer to them. In a similar way, God desires for us to "dine" with Him. He wants us to enjoy Him and to get to know Him better. Is this because He needs us? No, but He wants to be with us, and we need to be with Him. When we fellowship with God, we feel more secure because we sense His love for us in a greater way! When we spend time with God alone we feel much more significant because we realize we are friends with the God of the universe!

God does not speak directly of our need for security and significance in Scripture because He does not want us to make the mistake of trying to meet these needs ourselves. But this is exactly what many Christians are attempting to do through "self-love," and many Christian counselors are encouraging them to do it. Self-love is not biblical, and it will not meet our need for security and significance.

In 2 Timothy 3:1, Paul says that "in the last days difficult times will come." Then he goes on to describe the sinful characteristics of those difficult times. He mentions that "men will be lovers of self." Here is a clear indication in God's Word that self-love is not appropriate even though many Christian counselors say that it is. But as Paul Brownback says, "for the most part 2 Timothy 3 has been ignored by the proponents of self-love."[6]

The passage that many Christians who believe in self-love focus on is Matthew 22:39 where Christ says, "you shall love your neighbor as yourself." This verse appears to be a command not only to love one's neighbor, but to first love one's self. But this is not the case. The command is to "love your neighbor." Christ is saying that our love for our neighbor ought to equal our love for ourselves. He is not endorsing self-love; He is acknowledging that it is the natural human condition (see Eph. 5:29). Even a self-love proponent like Bruce Narramore admits that Matthew 22:39 does not teach self-love. He states in his book, *You're Someone Special,* "I believe . . . people are right when they tell us to love ourselves. But they are wrong in trying to base self-love on this passage."[7]

The fact is that the Bible never encourages self-love, because self-love doesn't work. It does not really meet our deepest needs. We truly want and need others to love and esteem us. We are never really satisfied with who we are or what we have accomplished until we are loved and esteemed by someone whom we love and esteem. Michael Reagan, the oldest son of former President Ronald Reagan, is an example of this truth. Listen to his words.

Bill, Rudy and I were the Outboard World Champions of 1967! I was ecstatic, and most everyone was dumbfounded. The press went crazy. A man ran up and kissed me on both cheeks. "I love you," he said. "Who are you?" I asked. "I'm the guy who bet thirteen bucks on you in the Calcutta and I just won ten thousand dollars." The next day the papers reported: "Reagan's Son Wins Outboard Championship." I felt that I had finally done something significant. I was certain that when Dad read about it in the papers he would say, "Doggone it, Mike, you're a world champion. I guess you've finally found your niche," and he, Nancy or Mom would welcome me with open arms because of my success. I never heard from them. I realized with despair that no matter what I did, it probably wasn't going to be enough to earn the acceptance I so desperately wanted.[8]

Self-love and love for others

There are well-intentioned believers who say that if we love ourselves, then we will have the reserve and the ability to love others. This sounds very logical and right but it is simply not true. Larry Crabb responds to this by explaining that

> many people . . . think that learning to love themselves first makes it possible to love someone else later. One practical problem with this plan is our bottomless need to feel loved. Once we start working to love ourselves, we never get around to loving others. We may learn to be more assertive with them, but we don't really love them.[9]

So, self-love is not biblical, nor will it meet our need for security and significance, nor will it enable us to love others more. Self-love is in no way the solution to low self-esteem. Rather, we need to know God intimately, recognize who we are in Christ, and serve Him with our lives.

A few years ago a psychologist appeared for a week on *Good Morning America.* I was pleasantly surprised to hear her say that "serving others" is an important key to a positive self-image. This surprised me because so many Christian counselors today encourage people to take care of themselves almost to the exclusion of others. But here was a secular counselor emphasizing the importance of serving other people. However, as good as this is, it is not good enough. Serving others is important, but who we are serving is most important.

That great missionary to India, William Carey, became deeply concerned about the attitude of his son, Felix. The young man went to India as a missionary but later resigned his work to accept an appointment from the King of Burma to be ambassador to India. In a letter to a friend, the elder Carey wrote, "Felix is shrivelled from a missionary to an ambassador."[10]

It is not enough for us to simply serve others in order to experience the level of security and significance that our hearts long for; we must serve the living God.

Now this does not rule out ministering to people. On the contrary, it is clear from the words of Christ to Peter that we serve Him by serving others (John 21:15–17). If we think that we are serving God and we are not ministering to people, we are fooling ourselves. But the focus of our service must always be Christ! We should look beyond the people we are serving and realize that what we do is ultimately a ministry to the Lord (Matt. 25:45). If we only serve people, or we make them the focus of our ministry, we are leaving ourselves wide open for disappointment and discouragement. If we serve Christ by serving others, then this will contribute to our security and significance.

The apostle Paul says in 2 Corinthians 4:5, "For we do not preach ourselves but Christ Jesus our Lord, and ourselves as your bondservants for Jesus' sake." I do not believe it is therefore mere coincidence that Paul also says later on in 2 Corinthians 11:5, "I consider myself not in the least inferior to the most eminent apostles." Paul was almost certainly using the phrase "eminent apostles" with tongue in cheek.[11] Nevertheless, it is very clear that Paul had high self-esteem and that he felt significant. He was not proud, but he felt important because of his service for Christ.

Having pointed out that who we serve is crucial, it is also important that we are in the niche that God wants us.

Some Christians today overemphasize *being* a Christian and some overemphasize *doing* what a Christian should do. Neither extreme is healthy or correct. In order to feel secure and significant, we must spend time just being with God, and we must also make time for doing what God wants us to do for Him. Both are important and should be balanced in our lives. This is easier said than done but this lack of balance is one reason so many Christians today do not feel significant or secure in Christ.

Now some may wonder if *significant* is just another word for "pride," so let's look at Romans 12:3 where Paul says, "Through the grace given to me I say to every man among you not to think more highly of himself than he ought to think."

Paul is referring to pride. *Pride* is thinking more highly of ourselves than we ought to think. Pride is the sinful attempt to boost one's sagging self-esteem by having an inflated view of one's self. Make no mistake about it, pride is sin (James 4:6). But *significance* is simply the acknowledgment that "I am somebody because of Christ." This is not pride, nor is it selfishness.

In Philippians 2:3 Paul warns, "Do nothing from selfishness or empty conceit, but with humility of mind let each of you regard one another as more important than himself."

Feeling that you are "somebody in Christ" is not the same as feeling you are more important than others. That is selfishness and it is sin. But feeling like somebody in Christ is exactly how God wants us to feel. His desire is for us to be secure and significant in Christ.

A great example of this truth is found in the life of Billy Graham. During a question and answer session at the Conference for Itinerant Evangelists in Amsterdam in 1983, a third-world evangelist shouted at Billy Graham, "Billy, if you were not white and an American, where would you be today?" A silence fell over the huge crowd of four thousand evangelists as they waited for Billy's response. Dr. Graham lovingly but firmly replied, "I am who I am by the grace of God." The entire auditorium broke out in applause.[12] Here was a man who was humble and unselfish, but clearly secure and significant in Christ. This is where we all need to be, and by the grace of God we can all get there!

Notes

[1] Josh McDowell, *His Image . . . My Image.* San Bernardino, CA: Here's Life Publishers, 1984, p. 41.

[2] Neil Anderson, *Victory Over the Darkness.* Ventura, CA: Regal, 1990, p. 95.

[3] Josh McDowell, p. 33.

[4] Don Matzat, *Power Religion.* Chicago: Moody Press, 1992, p. 255–56.

[5] See Neil Anderson's book, *Victory Over the Darkness,* for a more complete biblical list of who we are in Christ, pp. 45–47.

[6] Paul Brownback, *The Danger of Self-Love.* Chicago: Moody Press, 1982, p. 62.

[7] Bruce Narramore, *You're Someone Special.* Grand Rapids, MI: Zondervan, 1978, pp. 21–22.

[8] Michael Reagan, *On the Outside Looking In.* New York: Zebra, 1988, pp. 144–45.

[9]Larry Crabb, *Finding God.* Grand Rapids, MI: Zondervan, 1993, p. 114.

[10]Mary Drewery, *William Carey: Shoemaker and Missionary.* London, England: Hodder & Stoughton, 1978, p. 166.

[11]Ralph Martin, *II Corinthians, Word Biblical Commentary.* Waco, TX: Word, 1986, p. 342.

[12]Josh McDowell, p. 35.

18. Abuse

GINNY grew up overseas, the child of dedicated missionary parents who always sought to be diligent in their work and sensitive to the needs of their children.

Several years ago, when the family came home on furlough, Ginny found the courage to tell her mother about the sexual abuse that had been common in their overseas home. Unknown to the family, their male servant had frequently fondled and sometimes forced Ginny to have sexual intercourse. He told her to never tell and promised to blame and hurt her if reports of this activity ever became known.

Ginny's parents were shocked to hear this news and eventually found a Christian counselor for their daughter. The counselor was an older Christian man with excellent credentials and a good reputation. In his meetings with Ginny, the young girl was helped greatly as she worked to overcome the trauma of sexual abuse.

One morning, to the shock of everyone in the Christian community, the radio announced that the counselor had been arrested for taking "indecent liberties" with a young patient in the psychiatric hospital where he worked. The family found another counselor for their daughter. This time they chose a well-respected female psychologist who was understanding and sensitive but not very effective in helping Ginny with her hurts and anger. "Never again will I be able to trust men," Ginny told her counselor recently. "I have been hurt too much. I don't want to date, and I'm not sure I even want to change."[1]

If you or someone you love has been sexually abused, Ginny's story probably rings painfully true. You understand how she feels and why she feels that way. If you have been the victim of sexual abuse you know how terrible it is and how your life has been devastated by it. What you may not know is how to recover from it. You may have gone to extensive counseling or therapy and still be wondering if healing is truly possible.

Let me say at the outset that extensive healing is entirely possible. Don't give up or lose hope. It can happen, even for you! Nevertheless, healing from this kind of spiritual/emotional trauma usually does not come quickly or easily. The reason this is true relates to the nature of abuse.

When a person is abused, two things happen. First, that person's emotional security and significance is damaged. The longer and more severe the abuse, the greater and more extensive the damage. This is true whether the abuse is sexual, physical, or verbal.

Verbal abuse is probably the most common form of abuse. All of us have experienced it at one time or another in our lives, often from people about whom we care deeply. And verbal abuse can be incredibly devastating and damaging.

It is said that Bill Glass, the former pro football star and evangelist, once asked a thousand prison inmates the following question, "How many of you had parents that told you that you would end up in prison one day?" It is reported that almost everyone raised their hands.[2]

Words can be very powerful tools for either building people up or tearing them down. That is why Paul told the Ephesians,

> Let no unwholesome word proceed from your
> mouth, but only such a word as is good for edification
> according to the need of the moment, that it may give
> grace to those who hear. (4:29)

The term *unwholesome* was often used to refer to spoiled fish or fruit.[3] When rotten or putrid words are spoken, they do not "give grace to those who hear," building up people spiritually and emotionally. Rather, abusive words damage and sometimes destroy a person's emotional security and significance. This is a very real danger. In Galatians 5:15, Paul warned the Galatians about this when he wrote, "If you bite and devour one another, take care lest you be consumed by one another."

Paul obviously was not saying that the Galatians were literally biting and consuming one another.[4] But both verbally and with their actions they were tearing each other apart. Regardless of the type of abuse, the abused person's emotional security and significance is damaged, sometimes almost totally destroyed. But this is still only half of the total picture.

The second thing to happen when a person is abused is that the abused person finds it very difficult to trust. The loss of trust is particularly acute in regard to sexual abuse, because the abuser is often someone who had the trust of the abused. As I say this, I think of a young woman whose grandfather repeatedly molested her while she was growing up. When she went to her mother, her mother refused to believe her. This response from her own mother tore the fabric of her trust even more severely. As a result, she now finds it difficult to trust anyone.

Although the loss of trust is most obvious in someone who has been sexually abused, the fact is that any type of abuse causes an erosion in trust. And this is a serious problem because abuse leaves a person with his or her security and significance damaged—perhaps severely. So healing and growth need to take place. But they cannot without trust because "trust is crucial for growth."[5]

We cannot grow as people or as Christians without other people. We have to trust others and allow them to be part of our lives in order to grow. So the abused person is in a profound dilemma. One needs to heal and grow, but in order to do so, one must trust others. But because of one's damaged security and significance, trust is very difficult and at times almost impossible. The hopelessness of the situation often leads the abused person to deny that the abuse ever happened. Dan Allender points this out in his booklet, *When Trust Is Lost.*

> Abuse victims have an especially difficult time coming to terms with truth. Many have learned to live with their past by consciously or unconsciously pushing the abuse and pain from their memory. Denial was likely one of the chief means for surviving their abuse. Many victims find a crack in the wall to concentrate on during the abuse or learn to "leave their body" and soar away to a more pleasant place. Some develop multiple personalities in which to hide. Those patterns of disassociation often carry on today. Many make excuses for the perpetrator or the non-offending parent(s). "It wasn't his fault. I'm sure I did something to lead him on." Or, "I know my mother would have protected me, if she only knew."[6]

Victims of abuse often choose to deny rather than face the truth, because simple survival seems more attractive and possible than healing or growth. But it is crucial for healing that abused people recognize the painful truth and begin to deal with it.

There is much confusion and error today regarding the matter of denial. Abuse victims can, with God's help, remember if they were abused in the past, even if they have repressed or denied these memories for years. Many counselors today believe that only a trained professional can help an abused person recall repressed memories of abuse. Allender, for one, does not accept this. He says, "When we are willing to face the truth, . . . God will, in time, begin to bring back to memory all that we need to recall."[7]

There is growing evidence that suggests that victims sometimes recall incidents of abuse that never happened, or they believe a particular person abused them who in reality did not. There is also a growing concern that counselors and therapists are contributing to this problem by the ways in which they help people recover their repressed memories.[8]

Many abused people today are either repressing or denying the truth about the past. If these individuals want to recover and deal with the memories, professional aid may be helpful, but the Holy Spirit alone can lead them into truth. By asking Him to show them the truth, God will work effectively and graciously over time. Many victims of abuse, however, are not willing to face the past because their significance and security has been so damaged and their trust in others has been lost. But the most important reason why Christians refuse to face the truth of abuse has to do with God.

> A central question in the mind of the abused person, "Where was God?", compels many to answer by denying the influence of past events on present problems. If the past is insignificant, then I don't need to ponder the question, "Why didn't God intervene?" The unbelieving world is willing to see the damage of abuse, because it

feels no need to defend the God who could have inter-
vened to stop it. the Christian community, however,
feels disposed to deny any data that casts doubt on God's
presence or willingness to act for the sake of His children. "Where was God?" is a legitimate cry of the soul
to understand what it means to trust God.[9]

The question "Where was God?" is not only a "legitimate cry of the soul," but it is a question that must be
addressed. But is it being addressed? Over the past several
years I have read many articles and books about the subject of
abuse, and I have interviewed people who have been to counseling for abuse. During my exposure to this problem a disturbing pattern has emerged. Abused people do not want to
address the question "Where was God?", and neither do most
Christian counseling professionals. I'm sure that one reason
counselors do not want to broach this question has to do with
their sensitivity to the victim. This is a legitimate concern.
The issue of God's lack of intervention during abuse is something that should not be brought up quickly or inappropriately.
Nevertheless, it is an issue that has to be dealt with, and until
it is, healing and growth can only go so far.

How can a victim of abuse ever be truly secure if one is
not really sure that God loves him or her? How can an abused
person ever feel significant if he or she wasn't important
enough for God to step in and help? How can the abused individual trust and love a God who either doesn't care or is not in
ultimate control of all things? These questions have to be
answered eventually, even if the asking is painful and the
answer is not what the abused person wants to hear. This is
like surgery that is necessary to save a life, but the operation
and recovery is extremely painful. Surgery can be postponed
but it must eventually be undertaken, unless God wonderfully
and supernaturally shows His love for the person through the
life of another.

Antonio Sanchez was only five years old when he was sent to a Mexican prison for juveniles after allegedly murdering his baby brother. Tony's parents, who had beaten him with chains and tortured him with fire, deserted him and disappeared after telling police he was the killer. In prison other inmates taunted him with the word "murderer" and sometimes abused him. He had to fight for food.

No one seemed to care what happened to Tony, until Carolyn Koons, an American professor, heard his story. She battled bureaucracy and a corrupt prison warden for almost three years to secure Tony's release and adoption at age twelve; but her real struggles had only begun. Somehow she had to meet the needs of a boy who still stuffed rolls into his pockets because of past hunger, who lashed out at others because of his emotional scars, and who seemed enticed by every wrong because of his unbridled life. As a single parent, she was unsure whether she could meet his physical, emotional, and spiritual needs. But she did because she had a heavenly Father, unlike Tony's earthly one, who understood her needs.

Tony Sanchez was not initially drawn to his new mother. In fact, he seemed more drawn to trouble than to anything else. He accused her frequently of not loving him and taunted her with "I won't obey you or anyone." Carolyn never stopped barbecuing those juicy hamburgers he craved, never quit hugging him after his acid words, never ceased rescuing him from fights.

Carolyn had almost despaired of Tony ever bonding to her; somehow all those daily little things she had done for him seemed to have no impact. But then Carolyn got a big surprise; Tony made an unexpected speech at his junior high graduation. In almost a stutter he said, "I want to thank my mom for adopting me and bringing me to the United States." Then with tears streaming down his face, he yelled, "I love you, Mom. I love you. I love you."[10]

If you have been abused in any way, God may bring someone into your life who loves you so sincerely and unconditionally that you begin to realize God cares about you as well. If you recognize God's love for you in the life of a fellow Christian, you may begin to trust Him again and start to grow and heal. This is why it is so important to find a sensitive, loving, empathizing person to counsel and disciple you if you have been abused. But human empathy and unconditional love may still not be enough to restore trust between you and God. Because the question may still remain, If God really loves me why didn't He do something? For the answer to this question we need to take a close look at the book of Genesis, and in particular, the life of Joseph (Gen. 37–50).

Joseph was a person who experienced terrible betrayal and severe abuse. As a young man he was rejected by his own brothers, thrown into a pit by them, and then sold into slavery in Egypt. There he acted in a very responsible manner, but was the victim of an aggressive woman who tried to force herself on him. Even though Joseph repeatedly resisted her attempts to seduce him, he was rewarded for his efforts with a prison term.

There in prison he helped a man who promised to put in a good word for him to Pharaoh. But when the individual was released and reported for duty to Pharaoh, the promise was forgotten. But God had not forgotten Joseph, and with God's supernatural help, Joseph obtained the opportunity to serve Pharaoh. The result was that Joseph was made second in command only to Pharaoh himself, and was put in charge of saving Egypt from a coming famine. Joseph wisely stored up grain so that when the famine occurred he was prepared to feed not only Egypt, but people from all over the world. At this point, Joseph's brothers entered his life again. They were sent by their father to Egypt to buy grain because the famine was worldwide.

When the brothers arrived in Egypt, Joseph recognized them, but they didn't recognize him. This gave Joseph an opportunity to test them, which he did more than once, and see if they had changed. When Joseph was satisfied that his brothers were changed men, he revealed his true identity to them. They were petrified. But Joseph reassured them with these words, "Do not be grieved or angry with yourselves, because you sold me here, for God sent me before you to preserve life" (Gen. 45:5). Later on Joseph told them, "As for you, you meant evil against me, but God meant it for good in order to bring about this present result, to preserve many people alive" (Gen. 50:20).

The point of this true story about an abused and betrayed man is that God is working out His loving plan for us even in the midst of horrible situations.

Good out of evil

This is the promise of Romans 8:28, although the promise is not what a lot of Christians understand it to be. The verse says, "We know that God causes all things to work together for good to those who love God, to those who are called according to His purpose." It is important to understand that this verse is not saying that "God causes all things" that happen. Rather, it says that "God causes all things to work together for good." God is not evil and He does not cause evil things to happen to His children (Luke 11:11–13). But sometimes He does allow things to happen in our lives that are terrible and painful, but are ultimately for good. But what is the good? Verse 28 does not tell us, but the next verse does. "For whom He foreknew, He also predestined to become conformed to the image of His Son, that He might be the first born among many brethren" (8:29).

The good toward which God is working all things in our lives is Christlikeness. He wants us to be like His Son. This is

God's highest good, but it is also our highest good. As we become more like Christ we will experience what we have always longed for. Jesus Christ was the most secure and significant person who ever lived. He completely realized both the love that the Father has for Him and the significance that He has in the Father's eyes (Matt. 3:17). As we are conformed to the image of Christ we will realize more and more the Father's love and approval of us as well. Our deepest need for security and significance will be increasingly met as we love God and allow Him to work out His plan in our lives.

God does know what you have been through. He takes no pleasure or joy in the abuses that you have endured and He will hold the perpetrators accountable for their actions someday soon (Rom. 14:11–12). Nevertheless, He asks you to trust Him so that you can find what your heart truly longs for.

Summary

The question is this: "Do I believe that God is a loving Father who is committed to my deepest well-being, that He has the right to use everything that in me for whatever purposes He deems best, and that surrendering my will and my life entirely to Him will bring me the deepest joy and fulfillment I can know this side of heaven?"[11]

If your answer is "yes," I rejoice with you. You are on your way to growth and healing. You will still need time, counsel, and discipleship to experience the fullest of what God can do for you in this life. But you are on your way!

If your answer to the above question is "no," I don't condemn you. Nevertheless, I urge you to keep considering what God can do for you if you trust Him. I also encourage you to keep seeking someone to counsel you and love you with God's own love. Finally, and most importantly, I ask you to "consider Him who has endured such hostility by sinners against Himself, so that you may not grow weary and lose heart" (Heb. 12:3).

If you are struggling to trust God or if you are feeling that God is asking too much of you, let me humbly suggest that you fix your eyes on Jesus "so that you may not grow weary and lose heart."

Life is hard. Abuse can make it seem unbearable. The temptation is to deny what has happened and just try to survive or to refuse to trust anyone, including God. But neither survival nor isolation is a healthy, positive answer. The real answer is to first understand that God has a perfect loving plan for you and then trust Him to work it out. And if you begin to have doubts, keep your eyes on the Son!

Notes

[1] Gary Collins, *Case Studies in Christian Counseling.* Irving, TX: Word, 1988, p. 294.

[2] Dallas Seminary Sermon Illustration File.

[3] W. Baur, W. F. Arndt, F. W. Gingrich, *Greek-English Lexicon.* Chicago: U of Chicago Press, 1957, p. 749.

[4] Ibid., p. 169, 423.

[5] Dan Allender, *When Trust Is Lost.* Grand Rapids, MI: Radio Bible Class, p. 8.

[6] Ibid., p. 15–16.

[7] Dan Allender, p. 16.

[8] See, for instance, "A Question of Abuse," by Nancy Wartik in *American Health,* May, 1993; or "Making Monsters" by

[9] Dan Allender, *The Wounded Heart.* Colorado Springs: NavPress, 1990, p. 16.

[10] Haddon Robinson, *The Solid Rock Construction Company.* Grand Rapids, MI: Discovery House, p. 40.

[11] Dan Allender, *The Wounded Heart,* p. 175.

19. Marital Problems

IN the prologue to his book, *The Mystery of Marriage,* Mike Mason shares how he felt within days after his wedding.

> The week of our honeymoon, my wife and I stopped one afternoon at a Trappist monastery. It was a hot summer day, the air bright and still and the sky a deep, dusty blue. Nothing moved. There wasn't a monk in sight. We got out of our car and strolled hand in hand toward the monastery, and soon we emerged from the hot blue brightness of the day into the cool silent chapel, where there was a brightness of a different kind, and an interior stillness, too, that was quite different from the stillness outside. Our hands fell apart, and a feeling of awkwardness crept over me, an embarrassment. I suppose I was wondering what God really thought of this marriage of mine.
>
> We knelt to pray. The stillness clamored, echoed all over the building like shouts. It was reflecting my

heart, echoing back to me my own confusion. All the questions and doubts from the time of our engagement came rushing back. What was it all about, this marriage? And was it for real now? How could I have gone through with it? Was it really too late to back out? Who was this woman anyway? Couldn't I just stay here and become a monk? The silence of the chapel beat like wings all around us, but offered not one particle of consolation.

On the way out we met the guestmaster, a man who knew me. I introduced my new wife to him and felt ashamed. Certainly it would be all too clear to him, I thought, what a terrible mistake I had made. We exchanged pleasantries, then turned to go, and as we drove out the long treed lane that leads away from that beautiful place, I felt about as hopelessly trapped and as irredeemably desolate as I have ever felt in my life.[1]

During premarital counseling, I regularly inform engaged couples that at some point in their marriage each one will probably feel that a terrible mistake has been made. Usually this feeling does not occur during the honeymoon, but in some cases it does.

Sometimes a person senses that his or her marriage is a mistake due to fear of the unknown or the sudden realization that he or she is no longer free. But usually the feeling that something is dreadfully wrong comes as a result of marital discord or conflict, and this can occur at any point in a marriage. When marital problems grow severe enough, serious doubts about the marriage being right usually begin to develop in the minds of the couple. And even though they may seek counseling and strive to make the marriage work, the relationship is probably doomed unless their doubts are adequately addressed. This is why the first thing I deal with in marital counseling is the issue of whether or not the marriage is a mistake.

If a couple believes that it was sin or poor judgment that ultimately brought them together, then they will not be motivated to resolve their marital problems. They may make an attempt to go through the motions, and if they do the right things it is possible that the marriage may be saved. But the relationship will never really work well if deep down they still believe their union was a mistake.

On the other hand, if a couple believes that a loving God "who works all things after the counsel of His will" (Eph. 1:11) has ultimately brought them together, then they will be motivated to make their marriage good because they know that it can be good.

Now don't misunderstand what I am saying. I am not denying that people sometimes marry for sinful or foolish reasons. What's more, I am not saying that all marriages are ordained or arranged by God. But what I am affirming is that when two people are Christians or when God plans to draw them to Himself (John 6:44), their marriage is never, ultimately, a mistake or an unredeemable sin.

God does not cause us or want us to sin, nor does He cause us or desire for us to make foolish choices, but He is in absolute control of all things, including whom a Christian marries. Whomever He allows us to marry is in keeping with His eternal plan and purpose (Job 42:2).

It is true that God has told us that a Christian can marry anyone he or she wishes as long as that person is also a Christian (1 Cor. 7:39). We do in a very real sense have freedom as Christians to choose our mates. But God sovereignly arranges things so that whoever we marry, regardless of the reason or situation, is His choice as well as ours. J. Allan Peterson tells how he came to marry his wife and God's fingerprints are all over the story.

> Evelyn was a vivacious, gifted, generous, and popular girl when we first met. She had been engaged twice

before to Christian men and had no lack of admiring suitors. My first reaction upon recovering from the delightful shock of getting acquainted was, "I must rescue this girl from all her admirers." We became engaged— not that same day, of course, but not many months later. We both really wanted God's will in our lives and felt that He brought us together.

After a six-month engagement, we disagreed on whether to get married then or to go on to further schooling. We broke up completely. With finality, I went on to school. She returned to her home five hundred miles away. We maintained no contact and destroyed or returned all the mementos of our relationship, the letters, the pictures, rings, etc. And though we were totally out of each other's lives and greatly separated, I would often remember what a great girl she was and unconsciously compare my present dates to her. Evelyn still felt deep in her heart that God had brought us together originally, even though everything now indicated we would never see that happen.

Many months passed. Evelyn, coming to the conclusion that our friendship was totally gone, reluctantly made other plans. She took another job and her whole life headed in a different direction. Ultimately she met a fine Christian man and was engaged again and planned for their wedding. I had some reason to send her a note at this time, not knowing of her impending marriage to this good man—and, of course, not knowing that the invitations had been sent out, the showers given, the bridesmaids' dresses made, the minister engaged, and all the other preparations completed.

My note kindled an old flame. Her response awakened my appreciation of her. I made a telephone call. Her sparkling spirit captivated me again. The wedding was called off five days head of time and we picked up where we had left off. And there have been many side benefits. I still eat toast every morning from the toaster someone gave her for the other man!

Now I'm not suggesting this as a pattern. It was a pretty close call. But we both know and have never had a doubt that God brought us together to build a strong marriage and to help other marriages.[2]

For those of us who belong to God, there is no such thing as an accident or mistake. God will not allow us to do anything that cannot be worked out for His glory and our benefit. But in order for this to happen, we have not only to be "called according to His purpose," but to love Him as well (Rom. 8:28). And in order for us to love Him we have to believe that He is a wise, loving, all-knowing, and all-powerful God who wants what is best for us.

If you are experiencing marital problems, you need to decide what you believe about God. If He is not perfectly wise, then maybe a mistake was made. If He is not truly a loving God, then maybe He did give you your mate just to make you miserable! If God is not all-knowing and all-powerful, then perhaps He was not able to prevent you from making the biggest mistake of your life.

But if God is wise, loving, and in absolute control of all things, then you need to trust Him and do everything you can to work with Him in making your marriage work. You do have a part to play in your Christian growth (Phil. 2:12), and you also have a part in growing a Christian marriage. But your motivation and commitment to making your marriage work is directly tied to your view of God and His relationship to your marriage. This leads into the issue of what actually needs to be done.

Being all you can be

There are some key matters that must be addressed for a marriage to function properly and to be everything God intends. First, the husband and wife must each understand what the other needs and consciously attempt to meet that need on a regular basis.

Willard Harley in his book *His Needs, Her Needs* states that a man's "most basic need" in marriage is "sexual fulfillment," and a woman's is "affection."[3] Most men would probably agree with these conclusions because men do need sex. Most women, likewise, would affirm a need for affection. However, the biblical support for these conclusions is lacking. In Ephesians 5:33, Paul concludes his instructions to husbands and wives by saying, "Let each individual among you also love his own wife even as himself; and let the wife see to it that she respect her husband."

It would appear from this foundational passage regarding the marriage relationship that a husband's most basic need in marriage is for *respect,* and what his wife really needs is *love.* Let's explore the meaning and implications of this truth.

In chapter 17 of this book it was pointed out that both men and women have a divinely created need for emotional security and significance. What Ephesians 5:33 appears to indicate is that the greater priority for men is significance and for women the greater priority is security. What a man needs more than emotional security is respect. What a woman needs more than significance is love. Man and woman require both, but each has a priority for one or the other.

Paul commands husbands to love their wives "as their own bodies" (Eph. 5:28). He goes on to indicate that this involves nourishing and cherishing them (5:29). The word *nourish* has to do with providing for the physical needs of a person such as food and clothing.[4] The term *cherish* refers to meeting emotional needs. This word literally means to "keep warm."[5] Thus, the Scripture does not command the husband to have feelings of love for his wife. Rather he is commanded to love her by providing for her physical and emotional needs.

He is to make her feel secure by his actions, behavior, and words. This does not mean that he is free to be disrespectful to his wife. But above everything else she requires physical and emotional security from him.

Paul also commands the wife to "respect her husband" (Eph. 5:33). This relates to the issue of submission. Earlier in his discussion of the marital relationship, Paul says, "Wives be subject to your husbands, as to the Lord. For the husband is the head of the wife" (Eph. 5:22–23). This does not mean that wives should be slaves or doormats. Nor does this command prohibit wives from asking questions or making decisions. What submission does mean is that the husband has the last word about what goes on in the marital relationship and that he should be respected as the "head."[6] Although a husband needs emotional security, as does the wife, his greatest need is for significance.

Notice that the Bible does not say, "Husbands love your wives if they deserve it." Nor does it say, "Wives respect your husbands, if they have earned it." Rather, the Scriptures command us to do what is right, and it is in our best interest to do so.

Many husbands who are not receiving respect try to obtain it by threatening the security of their wives. These men erroneously think that they can scare their wives into respecting them. They may threaten to divorce their wives if they don't change or they threaten to cut off money for needed items or they may even threaten physical abuse. This simply diminishes whatever respect the wife has left for her husband and encourages even more disrespect. Threatening a wife's security only ensures that the husband's greatest need will not be met.

On the other hand, wives who are not being provided for physically or emotionally often try to gain security from their husbands by belittling them. These wives think that they can shame their husbands into loving them. So they call their husbands degrading names, publicly ridicule them, and nag them about all the things that they are not doing. Tragically, this simply reinforces the husband's thinking that his wife never appreciates anything he does for her. Shaming and nagging a husband just ensures that the wife's deepest need will continue to go unmet.

The right course of action for a husband is to consciously and regularly address his wife's need for security. If you're not sure what this means to your wife, ask her! Ask her what three specific things you could do regularly to show her that you love her. Whatever she asks (within reason) do it, and keep doing it! Eventually she will begin to respect you.

The same advice holds true for wives. Ask your husband what you can do to show him respect, and then do them. In time he'll begin to provide you with the security you need. I have found in working with couples that it usually doesn't take long for the other person to begin to respond positively to the other's efforts. But sometimes it does take time. This is often true when one's mate is not a believer, and it is also true when one's mate has an important need that has been seriously neglected in the past.

When a wife grows up in a home where she did not feel loved, for instance, she comes into the marriage needing a lot of security from her husband. But at the same time, because she feels her family failed her, she can tend to be very suspicious of her husband's attempts to love her. What's more, if he fails to effectively love her early in the marriage, she can become almost love resistant. She puts up a protective wall emotionally to keep herself from getting hurt any more. Of course, the same door that keeps hurt out, lets love in. This can also be an extremely frustrating situation for the husband who wants to provide emotional security for his wife. To help her overcome her resistance he will need to understand what has happened, not take it personally, and be very patient with his wife. It may take quite some time for her to let her husband past her self-protective barriers, but it can be done with God's help.

As important as it is for one to attempt to meet one's spouse's greatest need, it is equally important for one to address what the other fears the most. First John 4:18 says, "There is no fear in love, but perfect love casts out fear."

When a couple is experiencing marital problems, it is almost certain that fear is a factor. The husband may be attempting to love his wife, and the wife may be doing her best to treat her husband with respect. But the wife may still fear that as she grows older and loses some of her sex appeal, her husband may trade her in for a younger model. The husband, on the other hand, may be afraid that if he loses his job, for whatever reason, his wife may no longer respect him. The point is that a couple may be making a fine effort to meet each other's needs, and yet because of fear, they still experience marital discord and their security and significance is undermined. This is why couples need to use love to cast out fear. As each one taps into God's "perfect love," they are able to address what the other fears the most.

If the husband senses that his wife is afraid that he will leave her, he must regularly and verbally reassure her that he will never do so. If the wife figures out that her husband is afraid that he will lose his job, she needs to express her respect for his abilities and pledge her personal support of him. It is not enough to simply meet current needs, couples must also address future fears with love. But prayer is also a crucial factor in making a good marriage.

Prayer

There is a dissertation study that was done some years ago having to do with marital adjustment and prayer. Two separate groups of newly married couples were studied over a two-year period. In the first group, husbands and wives prayed with one another every day. In the second group, they did not. After the two years the couples that prayed together were better adjusted in their marital relationship by a significant margin.[7]

Prayer is also important in regard to marital communication. Many counselors encourage greater communication between couples and teach communication techniques. This is important. But prayer is of far greater significance.

In 1 Peter 3:7, Peter commands each husband to honor his wife as a "fellow heir of the grace of life, so that your prayers may not be hindered."

This is a difficult verse to interpret, but I believe God is saying prayer is an accurate barometer of the quality of the marital relationship. If the husband is treating his wife properly, "as a fellow heir of the grace of life," then he will be able to pray unhindered with his wife. But when the husband does not treat his wife as he should, then praying together is very difficult.

When couples are having marital problems I encourage them to pray very specifically for each other. The husband's prayer should include thanksgiving to God for his wife, specific requests for God's help in being a better husband, and specific prayer for his wife in regard to what she needs. The same pattern should be followed by the wife. This is not a time for subtle insults and veiled attacks. It must be positive and uplifting for both parties. If couples do this on a regular basis, it will transform both their relationship and their ability to communicate with each other. As H. Norman Wright says in *Romancing Your Marriage,* "Prayer . . . is the first step toward marital intimacy."[8]

Marital intimacy does not begin in bed, it begins next to the bed on one's knees in prayer with your mate. I cannot overstate the importance of prayer as both a barometer of a healthy relationship and as a means to greater communication and intimacy in marriage.

So, in order to deal with marital problems, a couple must first deal with doubts about the relationship being a mistake. Then a couple must seriously begin to meet each other's greatest need, and at the same time address what each fears, with love. And finally, a couple must establish the practice of praying together when building or rebuilding a marriage.

But what if your spouse still does not respond positively, and serious marital discord persists even after sincere effort over time on your part to meet needs, allay fears, and pray together? If this is the case, there is the very real possibility that your spouse is either disappointed or disillusioned with God.

Mike Mason believes that "when a man is no longer attracted to his wife, chances are that he will also have lost interest in his God."[9] From my counseling experience I would concur. Whenever a couple continues to have serious marital problems, I ask them at some point how their personal relationships with God are. Over the last ten years, without fail, they have admitted that it is not very good. It is hard to say whether a person's relationship with God, or one's relationship to one's spouse, goes first, but there is a very definite connection. Why is this the case?

First of all, there is no way to maintain a good marriage relationship today without God's help. There are too many factors working against it. The tremendous demands of work and children, extremely high marital expectations, the financial burdens, widespread substance abuse, and lack of support and encouragement from family and society at large are some of these factors.

But beyond this, when a marriage begins to develop serious problems, it takes a lot of strength and commitment to rebuild it. Without a close, personal relationship with God, neither spouse will have the emotional or spiritual reserves to put their marriage back together. All the best marital counseling, communication techniques, and high-powered analysis will be for naught if a couple does not draw close to God. People cannot have a good horizontal relationship if their vertical one is out of focus. This is why discipleship must take priority in rebuilding marriages. If a couple has severe marital problems and refuses to be discipled, apart from supernatural intervention, there is no hope. But when a husband or wife confess that their love for God has waned and are willing to work first and foremost on that relationship, there is all the hope in the world. Because with God all things are possible! (Luke 1:35).

Notes

[1]Mike Mason, *The Mystery of Marriage.* Portland, OR: Multnomah, 1985, p. 11.

[2]J. Allan Petersen, *The Myth of the Greener Grass.* Wheaton, IL: Tyndale, 1983, p. 70–71.

[3]Willard Harley, *His Needs, Her Needs.* Old Tappan, NJ: Revell, 1986, p. 10.

[4]W. Baur, W. F. Arndt, F. W. Gingrich, *Greek-English Lexicon.* Chicago: U of Chicago Press, 1957, p. 246.

[5]Ibid., p. 351.

[6]I am very aware of the ongoing debate about this word. But whether one interprets it as "first in rank" or "source," the connotation of "respect" still remains because of the context.

[7]Myron Freisen, "Marital Adjustment and Prayer." Unpublished D.Min. dissertation, Talbot School of Theology.

[8]H. Norman Wright, *Romancing Your Marriage.* Regal, 1987, p. 72.

[9]Mike Mason, p. 129.

Epilogue

A FRIEND of the late Teddy Roosevelt reported that he and Roosevelt used to play a little game when they were visiting each other. After an evening of conversation they would go outside on a clear night and search the skies until they found a faint speck of light-mist in a certain spot in the heavens. Then one or the other would recite:

> That is the Spiral Galaxy in Andromeda.
> That speck is as large as our Milky Way.
> It is one of a hundred million galaxies.
> It consists of one hundred billion suns, each larger than our sun.

Then Roosevelt would grin and say, "Now I think we are small enough! Let's go to bed!"[1]

Throughout this book I have sought to instill hope. I have attempted to address the problems that many readers are struggling with. I have tried to communicate that I am concerned, and more importantly, that the God of the universe cares about you and your difficult situation. But we need to get the big picture—the overall perspective with regard to our lives and our struggles. I also want to eliminate any possible misunderstanding about my view of God and His supreme importance.

As incredibly large as the universe is, the Bible shows that the entire universe is no bigger than God's out-stretched hand (Isa. 40:12). This gives us a picture of how great God is and how insignificant we are by comparison. That is why the psalmist wondered aloud, "What is man, that Thou dost take thought of him? And the son of man, that Thou dost care for him?" (Ps. 8:4).

It is wonderful that our God is so great and yet He cares so much for each one of us! And yet, we must constantly remember that God does not exist for us; we exist for Him and His glory. God is the source, sustainer, and goal of all things. This is why Paul says, "From Him and through Him and to Him are all things. To Him be the glory forever. Amen" (Rom. 11:36).

We must continually remind ourselves of this truth because if we don't we will not only end up profoundly disappointed, but we will inevitably fall into sin. God has left us here on earth for one overall purpose; to glorify Him in everything we do or say (1 Cor. 11:31). Our priority should not be on God's meeting our human needs, but rather on making our lives count for God and the cause of His Son, Jesus Christ!

Having once again swallowed that strong medicine, I am comforted by the psalmist's words, "He Himself knows our frame; He is mindful that we are but dust" (Ps. 103:14).

I am often amazed at God's thorough understanding of us as human beings and the way He accommodates Himself to our human needs and weaknesses. Take the issue of heavenly rewards for instance.

Even though there is considerable debate about the nature and extent of these rewards, it is clear from Scripture that these rewards are in addition to our eternal salvation (1 Cor. 3:14–15), and that God holds these heavenly rewards out to us as an incentive for faithful and righteous living (1 Cor. 9:24–27). Why would God do this?

Well, it is certainly not because He owes us anything, nor is it because we deserve them. The least we can do after He has so wonderfully and graciously saved us is to faithfully serve Him with our lives. And anything we accomplish for His glory in the process results from God's working in and through us (Phil. 2:13). Yet, God is willing to reward us for anything we do or say for Christ's sake (Mark 9:41).

The only answer is that God realizes that Christians require additional incentives to be faithful in serving Him. He has stooped to our human need and weakness and made an allowance for them. Is this legitimate and right? It must be or God would not do it. Oh, to be sure, God wants us to serve Him out of love and profound gratitude. God does desire for us to grow in regard to our motives for serving Him. But there is nothing wrong or immature about a Christian being motivated to serve God for heavenly rewards (1 Cor. 9:24–27). No Christian who is honest would state that he or she serves God exclusively for God's glory and benefit.

Years ago I heard Elisabeth Elliot confess publicly "Whenever I do something for God, it is always with mixed motives." Obviously, sinful motives are never acceptable to God, but it is clear that God expects us as human beings to be aware of and motivated by human need and desires, and that He is not opposed to this. He simply wants to be first in our lives, with us second.

There are vocal Christians today who insist that "felt needs" should not be addressed from the pulpit nor should Christians be concerned about their human needs. The emphasis and focus they say should be on God and God alone.

There is a certain amount of truth in this message. The Bible tells us not to be *anxious*—that is, unduly concerned—about our human needs (Matt. 6:31).[2] And it is also true that God should be the focus and priority of our lives. But to say that this excludes all discussion of "felt needs" or that God doesn't care about what we need is biblically wrong (Matt. 6:32). What God's Word says is that we should "seek first His kingdom and His righteousness; and all these things shall be added unto you" (Matt. 6:33). Based on this verse my concluding message to you is twofold.

First, as a struggling Christian you must make knowing and serving God the priority of your life. There is no way you can come to grips with your problems and become a whole person without doing this. Counseling is important, but even the best counsel will not be enough. You need to know God and you need to trust Him like you never have before. Personal wholeness is a by-product of knowing God and putting Him first in your life. There is no other way. Counseling may be a part of the healing process, but even the best counsel will never be enough.

Second, as you get intimately acquainted with God and live for Him first, your deepest human needs will be met, but perhaps not in the time or the way that you expected. You have to realize that getting to know the God of the universe is a life-long process. It is not easy for our finite minds to grapple with comprehending an infinite God. There is no quick fix; we must be patient.

When knowing and serving God begins to meet our deepest needs, it will not necessarily be the way in which we would plan it (Isa. 55:8–9). But we must continue to cling to God's promise,

> "For I know the plans that I have for you," declares the
> Lord, "plans for welfare and not for calamity to give
> you a future and a hope." (Jer. 29:11)

Notes

[1] Leslie Flynn, *Come Alive With Illustrations*. Wheaton, IL: Baker, 1987, p. 167.

[2] Charles Ryrie, *Ryrie Study Bible* (NIV). Chicago: Moody Press, 1986, p. 1719.

Selected Bibliography

Adams, Jay, *Competent to Counsel.* Grand Rapids, MI: Zondervan, 1986.

_____, *Christian Counselor's Manual.* Phillipsburg, NJ: Presbyterian and Reformed, 1973.

Allender, Dan, *When Trust Is Lost.* Grand Rapids, MI: Radio Bible Class, 1992.

_____, *The Wounded Heart.* Colorado Springs: NavPress, 1990.

Anderson, Neil, *The Bondage Breaker.* Eugene, OR: Harvest House, 1990.

_____, *Victory Over the Darkness.* Ventura, CA: Regal, 1990.

Augsburger, David, *The Freedom of Forgiveness.* Chicago: Moody Press, 1977.

Backus, William. *The Hidden Rift with God.* Minneapolis, MN: Bethany House, 1990.

Baker, Don and Emery Nester, *Depression: Finding Hope and Meaning in Life's Darkest Shadow.* Portland, OR: Multnomah Press, 1983.

Baur, W., Arnt, W. F., Gingrich, F. W., *A Greek-English Lexicon of the New Testament and Other Early Christian Literature.* Chicago: U of Chicago Press, 1957.

Barth, Markus, "Ephesians 4–6," *The Anchor Bible,* Vol. 34A. Garden City, NJ: Doubleday, 1974.

Beattie, Melody, *Codependent No More.* San Francisco: Harper, 1987.

Brown, Colin, ed., *New International Dictionary of New Testament Theology.* Grand Rapids, MI: Zondervan, 1975.

Brown, Francis, Driver, S. R., Briggs, C. A., *Hebrew and English Lexicon of the Old Testament.* Oxford, England: Clarendon Press, 1975.

Brownback, Paul. *The Danger of Self-Love.* Chicago, IL: Moody Press, 1982.

Bruce, F. F., *Commentary on Galatians*. Grand Rapids, MI: Eerdman's, 1982.

Collins, Gary. *Can You Trust Psychology?* Downers Grove, IL: InterVarsity Press, 1988.

_____, *Case Studies in Christian Counseling*. Irving, TX: Word, 1988.

Crabb, Larry, *Finding God*. Grand Rapids, MI: Zondervan, 1993.

_____, *Understanding People*. Grand Rapids, MI: Zondervan, 1987.

_____, and Dan Allender. *Encouragement: The Key to Caring*. Winona Lake, IN: BMH Books, 1986.

Dallas Seminary Sermon Illustration File

Dallimore, Arnold. *Spurgeon: A New Biography*. Carlisle, PA: The Banner of Truth, 1985.

Drewery, Mary, *William Carey: Shoemaker and Missionary*. London, England: Hodder & Stoughton, 1978.

Drummond, Lewis and Baxter, *How To Respond to a Skeptic*. Chicago: Moody, 1986.

Flynn, Leslie, *Come Alive With Illustrations*. Wheaton, IL: Baker, 1987.

_____, *The Sustaining Power of Hope*. Wheaton, IL: Victor, 1985.

Freisen, Myron, "Marital Adjustment and Prayer." Talbot School of Theology, unpublished D.Min. dissertation.

Guthrie, Donald. *Galatians*. Grand Rapids, MI: Eerdman's, 1981.

Hansel, Tim, *When I Relax I Feel Guilty*. Elgin, IL: David C. Cook, 1988.

Harley, Willard, *His Needs, Her Needs*. Old Tappan, NJ: Revell, 1986.

Hawkins, Don, Meier, Paul, Minirth, Frank, *Worry-Free Living*. Nashville, TN: Thomas Nelson, 1989.

Hiebert, D. Edmond, *The Epistle of James.* Chicago: Moody Press, 1979.

_____, *The Thessalonian Epistles.* Chicago: Moody Press, 1971.

Ice, Thomas and Robert Dean. *A Holy Rebellion.* Eugene, OR: Harvest House, 1990.

Jackson, Tim, *When Help Is Needed.* Grand Rapids, MI: Radio Bible Class, 1993.

Johnston, J. Kirk, *Why Christians Sin.* Grand Rapids, MI: Discovery House, 1991.

Lightfoot, J. B., *The Epistle of St. Paul to the Galatians.* Nashville, TN: Thomas Nelson, 1989.

Kirwan, William, *Biblical Concepts for Christian Counseling.* Grand Rapids, MI: Baker, 1984.

Knight, George W., *Commentary on the Pastoral Epistles.* Grand Rapids, MI: Eerdman's, 1992.

Koch, Kurt, *Occult Bondage and Deliverance.* Grand Rapids, MI: Kregel, 1972.

Kushner, Harold, *When Bad Things Happen to Good People.* Avenal, NJ: Outlet Books, 1986.

Harris, R. Laird, Archer, Gleason L., Jr., Waltke, Bruce K.,*Theological Workbook of the Old Testament.* Chicago: Moody Press, 1980.

MacArthur, John, *Our Sufficiency in Christ.* Irving, TX: Word, 1991.

Martin, Ralph, *II Corinthians, Word Biblical Commentary.* Waco, TX: Word, 1986.

Mason, Mike, *The Mystery of Marriage.* Portland, OR: Multnomah Press, 1985.

Matzat, Don, *Power Religion.* Chicago: Moody Press, 1991.

McDowell, Josh, *His Image . . . My Image.* San Bernardino, CA: Here's Life, 1984.

_____, *The Secret of Loving.* Wheaton, IL: Tyndale, 1986.

Minirth, Frank and Walter Byrd. *Christian Psychiatry.* Old Tappan, NJ: Revell, 1990.

Montbleau, Wayne, *The Wounded Healer.* Old Tappan, NJ: Revell, 1979.

Narramore, Bruce, "The Therapeutic Revolution," *Christianity Today,* May 17, 1993.

_____, *You're Someone Special.* Grand Rapids, MI: Zondervan, 1978.

Needham, David. *Birthright.* Portland, OR: Multnomah Press, 1979.

Peterson, J. Allan, *The Myth of the Greener Grass.* Wheaton, IL: Tyndale, 1983.

Playfair, William, *The Useful Lie.* Wheaton, IL: Crossway, 1991.

Reagan, Michael, *On the Outside Looking In.* New York: Zebra, 1988.

Rienecker, Fritz, *A Linguistic Key to the Greek New Testament, Vol. 2.* Grand Rapids, MI: Zondervan, 1980.

Robinson, Haddon, *The Solid Rock Construction Company.* Grand Rapids, MI: Discovery House, 1988.

Ryrie, Charles, *Basic Theology.* Wheaton, IL: Victor, 1986.

_____, *Ryrie Study Bible* (NIV). Chicago: Moody Press, 1986.

Sloat, Donald, *The Dangers of Growing Up in a Christian Home.* Nashville, TN: Thomas Nelson, 1986.

Smedes, Lewis, *Forgive & Forget.* San Francisco: Harper, 1984.

Smith, Fred, *Learning to Lead.* West Orange, NJ: Leadership Library, 1986.

Springle, Pat, *Overcoming Codependency.* Dallas: Rapha, 1990.

Sproul, R. C., *The Hunger for Significance.* Ventura, CA: Gospel Light, 1991.

Stoop, David and Stephen Arterburn, *The Angry Man.* Irving, TX: Word, 1991.

Stott, John R. W., *The Message of II Timothy.* Downers Grove, IL: InterVarsity Press, 1973.

Strauss, Lehman, *In God's Waiting Room.* Grand Rapids, MI: Radio Bible Class, 1984.

Strommen, Merton, *Five Cries of Youth.* San Francisco: Harper, 1988.

Szasz, Thomas, *The Myth of Mental Illness.* New York: Dell, 1960.

Tada, Joni Eareckson, *Choices and Changes.* Grand Rapids, MI: Zondervan, 1986.

Toussaint, Stanley and Charles Dyer, ed., *The Traitor in the Gates: The Christian's Conflict with the Flesh.* Essays in Honor of J. Dwight Pentecost, Chicago: Moody Press, 1986.

White, John. *The Masks of Melancholy.* Downers Grove, IL: InterVarsity Press, 1982.

Wright, H. Norman, *Romancing Your Marriage.* Ventura, CA: Regal, 1987.

Note to the Reader

The publisher invites you to share your response to the message of this book by writing Discovery House Publishers, P. O. Box 3566, Grand Rapids, MI 49501, U.S.A. or by calling 1-800-653-8333. For information about other Discovery House publications, contact us at the same address and phone number.